Signing Italian/American Cinema

A More Focused Look

Anthony Julian Tamburri

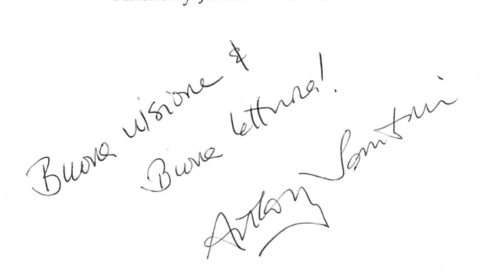

OVUNQUE SIAMO PRESS

Library of Congress Control Number: Available upon request.

Cover image from *Dinner Rush,* "The Godfather's Table"
Used with kind permission from GIRALDIMEDIA
http://giraldi.com

Printed in the United States.

Published by
OVUNQUE SIAMO PRESS
Ambler, PA

ISBN 978-1-7339948-2-8

"[I]n the darkness you find two seats ... and go lifting, speeding into the great moving magic of the silver screen which pulls all into itself, lulling with the magnetic other-worldliness all who sit in adoration before it. [...] And here people can lose their identity in a splurge of altruism before the twentieth century god. His messengers, his missionaries are everywhere."

—Sylvia Plath,
The Unabridged Journals of Sylvia Plath

"Michael Cimino depicts an incident in The Sicilian *that would have been instructive if it had been able to convey to an American audience the economic plight of Sicily in the post-World-War-II years. Instead, it merely generated snickers in the audience when I saw the film.*"

—Ben Lawton
"America through Italian/American Eyes:
Dream or Nightmare?"

TABLE OF CONTENTS

vii • Acknowledgments

1 • Visuality And Its [Dis]Contents: Looking Backward in Order to Move Forward

15 • Old World versus New. Or, Opposites Attract: Emanuele Crialese's *Nuovomondo*

51 • Viewing *Big Night* as Easy as One, Two, Three: A Peircean Notion of an Italian/American Identity

73 • Food as Delineator in *Dinner Rush*: A Semiotic of Generational Difference among Italians in America

95 • Signing Italian/American Cinema, Code-switching in the City: What Does Scorsese Mean in *Mean Streets*?

113 • Conclusion

119 • Index

127 • About the Author

ACKNOWLEDGEMENTS

The essays in this study have already appeared in print in either English or Italian. Chapter 1, "Old World versus New. Or, Opposites Attract: Emanuele Crialese's *Nuovomondo*," first appeared in my *Re-viewing Italian Americana: Generalities and Specificities on Cinema* (2011); it appears here slightly modified. I decided to include it in this collection precisely because it congeals with basic semiotic tenets and resonates in what some might consider the intentionality of this book, which is to engage in a more systematic semiotic analysis of the potentiality of signification in the films examined herein. Chapter 2, in turn, "Viewing *Big Night* as Easy as One, Two, Three: A Peircean Notion of an Italian/American Identity," was published in the online journal *Luci e ombre* 3.1 (Jan.-Mar 2015). It represents the culmination of notions of identity as expressed by both Charles Sanders Peirce and Irvin Child, two seemingly divergent theorists of different disciplines who, nevertheless, prove compatible in this setting, as they each speak to notions of identity and individual cognition. Chapter 3, "Food as Delineator in *Dinner Rush*: A Semiotic of Identity and Generational Difference among Italians in America," was delivered as a keynote lecture at the conference "Politiche del gusto: mondi comuni, fra sensibilità estetiche e tendenze alimentari," in Palermo, 2 December 2018; it subsequently appeared in the online journal of the Associazione Italiana di Studi Semiotici (Italian Association of Semiotic Studies). Finally, chapter 4, "Signing Italian/American Cinema, Code-switching in the City: What Does Scorsese Mean in *Mean Streets*?," appears here for the first time in English, slightly modified from its Italian version, "Il sistema di segni del cinema italiano/americano: *code-switching* e la significabilità di *Mean Streets* di Martin Scorsese," *Ácoma* (Fall-Winter 2017): 108-121.

Along the way, a few essays penned by others have appeared on the films I discuss here. In some cases, these subsequent studies have made further contributions to the interpretation of said films.

"Acknowledgements"

When this occurred and where there was overlap, as there shall always be, I have scrupulously cited those essays and tried to engage with them in my respective chapters. Where, in turn, there was nothing new, I have opted not to engage them; I shall reserve that task for a more suited venue, as I did regarding literary criticism on Italian/American texts.

As I have repeatedly stated in other venues, no book is ever completed in a vacuum; there is always someone with whom we share our ideas and/or who serves as our sounding board. A few people have been instrumental in this case. As always, Maria afforded me the time to write. From the editors of the journals in which two of these essays appeared to the friends who read previous drafts of my essays, I would like to thank the following: Ryan Calabretta-Sajder, Fred Gardaphé, Paolo Giordano, Donatella Izzo, Ben Lawton, Joseph Sciorra, Sabrina Vellucci, and Antonio Vitti. I wholeheartedly thank them all.

Any real and/or perceived fallacies are my own.

INTRODUCTION

Visuality And Its [Dis]Contents:
Looking Backward in Order to Move Forward

The essays in this book all share a common notion that a greater awareness of the potentiality of signification of sign functions is an indispensable tool for a more extensive understanding of how a film might signify—indeed, about how any text might signify. That said, I should state here at the outset that my use of the binomial "extensive understanding" is by no means evaluative; my only intention is to underscore that through semiotics and its various components of interpretation we can testify to the greater potentiality of signification that any text—e.g., cinematic, written, figurative—may produce with respect to a more conventional analytical process that, as well, does not take into consideration secondary or tertiary functions of the signs in question.

The field of visuality still remains a complex arena of intellectual interrogation in spite of a plethora of books that have appeared. The study of visual communicative processes calls for a theory and methodology that are both multi-disciplinary and multidimensional in performance; people who write on this topic come from mass communication, film and cinema studies, education, art, anthropology, literature, psychology, architecture, philosophy, linguistics, and semiotics, among other fields.

One might surely go back to the studies of perceptual psychology via the likes of Erwin Panofsky and his three strata of subject matter (1972), or Rudolf Arnheim and his notions 1) that perception and thinking are strongly related and 2) that, as well, form and content are intrinsically connected.[1] They laid the groundwork for pro-

---

[1] For Erwin Panofsky I have in mind his canonical *Studies in Iconology* (1972), *Meaning in the Visual Arts* (1955), as well as his "Style and Medium in the Motion Pictures" (1995 [1936]). For Rudolf Arnheim, in turn, I would note *Art and Visual Perception* (1954), *The Power of the Center* (1982), and *Film as Art* (1955).

1

vocative and innovative studies in art history that went beyond—
some might say transgressed—foundational notions of intentionality
that undergirded the field of art history through the early twentieth
century.

I have opted predominantly for a semiotic analysis of the films
herein for reasons that will become clear as one reads further. Ad-
ditionally, such an approach has informed previous arguments of
mine dedicated both to literature and cinema. In so doing, we can
take a step backward in order to move forward.[2]

In adopting the semiotic notions of Charles Sanders Peirce,
which are grounded in logic and cognition, as compared to the
structuralist concepts of de Saussure, which are in turn grounded
more in linguistics, one is afforded a much more liberating experience in his/her interpretation of the text at hand, as we shall see. It
is the very difference in each scholar's notion of the sign that con-
vinces me that Peirce's notion of the tripartite sign, as compared to
de Saussure's notion of the bipartite sign, allows for the more ex-
pansive experience of textual interpretation and hence greater signifying potentiality of the signs in question.

In her intriguing 1973 study on visuality, *A Primer of Visual Literacy*, Donis A. Dondis tells us that "[v]isual expression is many things,
in many circumstances, to many people. It is the product of highly
complex human intelligence of which there is pitifully little understanding" (9). Dondis may not be all that wrong about notions of visuality in a general sense and, especially, for her time. Arnheim and
Panofsky were pioneers in this arena. They moved away from traditional art history steeped in authorial intention (read, also, painter,
sculptor, etc.), chronology, categories, labeling, and the like. Their respective legacies lie—to varying degrees—in the works of Mieke Bal,
Norman Bryson, Michael Anne Holly, Martin Kemp, Griselda Pol-
lock, and other like scholars who brought Marxism, semiotics, gender studies, queer theory, etc. to this new brand of art history. Indeed, one of the pioneer books is the 1988 title, *The New Art History*,
edited by A. L. Rees and Frances Borzello.

---

[2] My essays I am referencing here are 1990, 1994, 2015, 2017.

With regard to film criticism, we can see an analogous development, though much more abbreviated, given that film is born at the end of the nineteenth century, and hence a younger area of intellectual interrogation. Thus, academic film criticism—to distinguish it from the writing of many competent journalists—comes to light immediately after WW II with the likes of Andre Bazan writing for *Cahiers du Cinéma*; the French, in fact, will be dominant early on in the twentieth century. In the U.S., we can consider the anthology *Film Theory and Criticism* a first manifestation of the "growing interest in film theory and to the practice of a more rigorous criticism," as the editors wrote at the time (1974, ix). So that while these and other scholars are already engaging in film theory and criticism, the academic component of critical thought on film begins to organize itself with the Purdue University Annual Conference on Film, which held its first conference in March 1976 with annual meetings through 1983.

From Purdue's annual conferences a plethora of youngish scholars made their bones in film studies and went on to have prolific and influential careers. Some names that come to mind are: J. Dudley Andrew, Peter Bondanella, David Bordwell, Frank Burke, Herb Eagle, Jim Franklin, Anna Lawton, Ben Lawton, James Monaco, Armand Pratt, Janet Staiger, and others. At the same time, the Center for Twentieth Century Studies at the University of Wisconsin–Milwaukee had organized "two scholarly meetings" devoted to film, because the "movies"—to use Panofsky's terminology (Panofsky 1995, 94)—as Michel Benamou stated in his introduction to a special issue of *Quarterly Review of Film Studies*, "[are] artistic and technological alternative[s] to the print culture that has so long dominated the Western World" (1976, 7-9).[3]

The importance of these early, annual conferences on film studies and the trials and tribulations of teaching and studying film in that period are best summed up by Peter Bondanella in the preface

---

[3] Some of the names appearing here in both Part One and Part Two include: Stephen Heath, Seymour Chatman, Geoffrey Nowell-Smith, Robert Scholes, Gerald Mast, and others, some of whom also attended the Purdue University Conference on Film.

to his *A History of Italian Cinema*: "Before the age of DVDs and vide-
otapes, Ben Lawton … and I drove to the Indianapolis airport each
week when we both taught our film classes, swapping prints to
screen before they had to be sent back to the distributors. [...] Everyone in American universities and colleges interested in this subject
eventually gathered at the film conferences Ben organized at Purdue
over the years" (xiii).[4]

Returning to Dondis, we see that she continues later in her
study to affirm, if ever so briefly, that, in film, "the dominant visual
element is movement" for both the filmmaker and the spectator.
Dondis is not alone with regard to the notions of movement as
dominant characteristic and that of filmmaker and spectator as, to
varying degrees, collaborators in the enjoyment and/or signifying
reception of film. Close to forty years before, Erwin Panofsky articulated similar notions in his essay "Style and Medium in the Motion Pictures." He stated: "primordial basis of the enjoyment of
moving pictures was … the sheer delight in the fact that things
seemed to move" (93). He then continued: "movement to works of
art [that were] originally stationary [… did not intrude] upon the
sphere of higher culture" (95). What the advent of film then did was
not to supplant one art for another; rather, film added yet another
art form in the ever-developing world of visuality, and at a more
popular level "without intruding upon … higher culture."

The experience of spectatorship is new with the advent of film.
Panofsky tells us that in theater, for example, "space is static, that
is, the space represented on the stage, as well as the spatial relation
of the beholder to the spectacle, is unalterably fixed. The spectator
cannot leave his seat, and the setting of the stage cannot change"
(96). With regard to film—"the movies," the term Panofsky persists
in using herein—"the situation is reversed" (96); while it is true that
the spectator in film also "occupies a fixed seat," s/he does so "only
physically, [and] not as the subject of an aesthetic experience" (98).
Panofsky then continued:

---

[4] I owe a debt to Ben Lawton for his invaluable assistance in this brief history of the begin-
nings of film criticism in the United States.

Aesthetically, [the spectator] is in permanent motion as [her/his] eye identifies itself with the lens of the camera, which permanently shifts in distance and direction. And as movable as the spectator is, as movable is, for the same reason, the space presented to [her/him]. Not only bodies move in space, but space itself does, approaching, receding, turning, dissolving and recrystallizing as it appears through the controlled locomotion and focusing of the camera and through the cutting and editing of the various shots—not to mention such special effects as visions, transformations, disappearances, slow motion and fast-motion shots, reversals and trick films. (98)

The spectator of the movies, then, is in motion with the dynamics of the film as the narrative unfolds. Indeed, Panofsky anticipates here future discussions that will develop around the notion of the 'gaze' insofar as the spectator's "eye identifies itself with the lens of the camera" and hence, in its scanning of all that occurs on screen, presumably also 'objectifies' what it sees (e.g., "bodies") during its act of signification. My use of the word "objectify" has two referents here. First, with regard to signification, it dates back to Peirce and his notion of the sign for which one of its components is indeed the "object" of the representamen in his triangle of the sign:

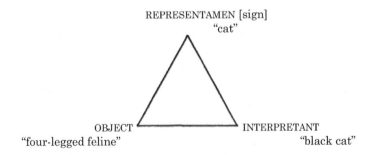

REPRESENTAMEN [sign]
"cat"

OBJECT
"four-legged feline"

INTERPRETANT
"black cat"

Namely, one passes from the primary stage of the concept to a mental image of said concept; hearing the word "cat" ("representamen"), one creates a mental image of a four-legged feline ("object"). Each individual, however, may very well have a specific mental image of the "object" in question, the four-legged feline: one may think of a black cat, another a white cat, and so on ("interpretant").[5]

The second referent is the more recent notion of treating someone — usually in reference to women — as an 'object,' in that such an act depersonalizes the individual being watched as if s/he had no feelings, opinions, or, more significant, no rights of her/his own. The use of the word "gaze" in this second instance also brings us back, first and foremost, to Jean Paul Sartre's *Being and Nothingness*, in which he discusses the gaze as an objectifying act, one that can also dehumanize (1993 [1943]). Eventually, through Michel Foucault (1973, 1979 [1975]), as a fundamental voice, we arrive at Laura Mulvey's notion of the second-wave feminist concept of "male gaze" (1975).[6]

Returning now to Panofsky's quote above, we read that the spectator's own actions are in concert with the phenomena of the film and all it pertains; and this includes, especially, the actions of the director and various editors involved in bringing to the screen the finished product: "through the controlled locomotion and focusing of the camera and through the cutting and editing of the various shots — not to mention such special effects as visions, transformations, disappearances, slow motion and fast-motion shots, reversals and trick films." Both spectator and filmmaker, then, are responsible for the production of meaning of the film in question.

Dondis continues to affirm that film not only replicates reality but it can indeed "carry information and deliver it in the most realistic manner" (175). Panofsky had already articulated something similar: the controlled locomotion mentioned above "opens up a world of possibilities" for which "there is, on the purely factual

---

[5] Peirce defines this triadic relationship as follows: "A REPRESENTAMEN is a subject of a triadic relation TO a second, called its OBJECT, FOR a third, called its INTERPRETANT, this triadic relation being such that the REPRESENTAMEN determines its interpretant to stand in the same triadic relation to the same object for some interpretant" (Peirce 1.541). For more on Peirce, see his *Collected Papers* (1931-1935).

[6] Mulvey's notion has been subsequently both reinforced and challenged over the years. For more on this and a further developed notion of the gaze as multi-layered and no longer male only, see Ryan Calabretta-Sajder.

level, an untold wealth of themes" (98). This very notion that a film can not only replicate reality, and hence satisfy in a casual and basic manner a spectator's expectations, but a film may indeed carry — and here I would add 'other' (read also, additional) — information than the expedience of the notion of what Dondis labels a "realistic manner." That is, as we shall see in the essays herein — like any text — a film may indeed possess certain visual qualities — for instance, secondary images and/or utterances — that add to a greater signifying potentiality of the film in question, as I would submit, Panofsky intimates.

<p

In addition to all that we have discussed above, there is also, as some have indicated, the pre-filmic phenomena of (a) choosing which film to see, (b) relying on one's basic recognition of the generic rhetoric of cinema and all that it pertains, (c) the viewer's emotional expectations as the lights dim in the movie house, and (4) the viewer's willingness to allow him/herself to be transported into the "reality" of the screen.[7] At this juncture, I might pause to admit my realization that some might think that I am speaking a bit anachronistically; for with the onset of computers and smart phones, and all the technology that has accompanied such inventions, one might indeed ask, "Who goes to the movies anymore?" While the question is a valid one, for sure, I would question its over-expansive reach. Films, I would submit, are still produced for the "big screen," many of which can still be better appreciated in a movie theater than on one's computer or smart phone, especially if we are talking about a first-time viewing that is, as usually the case, for entertainment purposes.

In 1963, Italo Calvino offered his reader a wonderful description of Marcovaldo's movie-going experience.[8] Marcovaldo is a countryman, an unskilled laborer who finds himself in the city, and in an attempt to escape the toils of his daily grind, he often concocts

---

[7] I am borrowing here, in part, from Lauro Zavala (1994, 15). In this section of his book he is speaking to the figure of the "espectador casual" (casual spectator).
[8] I am quoting from the English translation (1983).

schemes that might reify his fantasies. In the end, however, they most always seem to fail him. In one story, "The Wrong Stop," Marcovaldo projects his ideas onto a giant screen that is, first, the screen in a movie theater, and, second, once he exits the movie theater, the "thick, opaque fog, which engulfed things and sounds, flattened distances into a space without dimensions, mixed lights into the darkness and transformed them into glows without shape or place" (60-61). Thrust into a formless world of daydreams, just like the casual movie goer who allows him/herself to be transported into the "reality" of the screen, Marcovaldo takes a tram presumably headed for home, but, losing himself in his own 'imagined' world of India, a continuation of sorts of what he saw in the movie theater, he loses count and gets off the tram at the wrong stop. With Marcovaldo unaware of where he is, Calvino describes Marcovaldo's temporary dilemma as the "perfect situation for day dreaming, for projecting in himself, wherever he went, a never-ending film on a boundless screen" (61). For the casual viewer, then, this is the usual experience in the movie theater, to lose oneself into the reality of the film, to find that "perfect situation for day dreaming, for projecting in himself … a never-ending film on a boundless screen," as Calvino wrote close to sixty years ago.

This is also, as I have demonstrated elsewhere, what Marcovaldo indeed does.[9] The city he traverses consists mainly of fog and, literally, voids—empty spaces in the dark, similar, though not identical, to those Iserian blanks that he, like the reader of any problematic text, attempts to fill. For Wolfgang Iser, a blank is "suspended connectability in the text" (1980, 198), which, by nullifying "good continuation" and mobilizing the reader's imagination, nevertheless increases "the constitutive activity of the reader who cannot but try and supply the missing links that will bring the schemata together" (186). While their functions are not identical, we may see an analogy in Calvino's fog, and voids literally serve as "suspended connectability in the text," and "the resultant break in good continuation intensifies the acts of ideation on the reader's part, and in this respect

---

[9] I am borrowing here from a previous study of mine on Calvino's *Marcovaldo*. (2003).

the blank functions as an elementary condition of communication" (189). That is, the reader — as well as Marcovaldo the viewer — must now confront what s/he has perceived so far through the dominant narrative pattern with those images, or modifications of images, now offered by the blanks. Lest we forget that Marcovaldo had seen a film about India, and that he "would see the picture twice, ... and in his thoughts he continued living in those landscapes and living those colors" (60). It was itself a foggy film, about a forest in which "steam rose in clouds from the swampy undergrowth" (60). These, we might contend, constitute Marcovaldo's fore-understanding, his "anterior relation to the subject" of the text that is herein the dark, shadowy, foggy city that Marcovaldo now has to negotiate.[10] In so doing, he is confronted with a number of obstacles that appear under the guise of thick fog, indistinguishably blurred images, faded lights, voids, and the like. He has thus become, at this juncture, a type of informed viewer, he has acquired some knowledge that his cultural reservoir now contains, which then will serve him in his greater "understanding" of the visual text.

Marcovaldo eventually does fill in these voids, willy-nilly, in an Iserian and Calvinian manner. In the "coming together of the text and [Marcovaldo's] imagination," to paraphrase Iser, Marcovaldo, through trial and error in his attempt to get home — that is, fill in the voids — ends up on an airplane to India. We should remember, at this time, that Marcovaldo, in exiting the theater, colored this initial void with the "images of India, the Ganges, the jungle, Calcutta" (61); in his thoughts, Calvino tells us, "he continued living in those landscapes and breathing those colors" (60). Such notions, of course, echo Calvino's earlier expression of the decisive moment of literary life as that of reading, for which literature holds a "'place'

---

[10] See Hans-Georg Gadamer and his notion of the hermeneutic circle (1988, 262). As has been pointed out by Richard Berstein, the hermeneutic circle has proven important also for understanding the sciences (1983, 131-138). Significant, then, with regard to the oscillation between parts and the whole are: 1) Paul Feyerabend's "anthropological method" for which "each block of information is a building block of understanding," only to be "clarified by the discovery of further blocks" (1975, 251), and 2) the process Clifford Geertz considers a "continuous dialectical tacking between the most local of local details and the most global of global structures in such a way as to bring both into view simultaneously" (1979, 239).

of privilege within the human consciousness" (16) from which the potentialities of a sign system may be, or are, eventually actualized. Marcovaldo, to be sure, in continuing to live and breath his exotic India outside the movie theater, actualizes the sign system of his cinematic dream world and ends up not on a tram headed toward Via Pancrazio Pancrazietti, but on a plane for Bombay, Calcutta, and eventually Singapore.

Now, while I consider Marcovaldo a type of "informed" viewer, I do not see him as the "specialized" viewer who might be capable of decoding the text according to what some might see as a "correct" and/or "adequate" interpretation. He is not, that is, the "espectador especializado" (47) that Zavala and others might want to see.[11] This viewer, we are told, would be conversant with systems and processes of signification, s/he would be an academic, for lack of a better term. He is the casual viewer, I would submit, who possesses some knowledge about the "film" in question, but not enough to fill in all the blanks. The distinction here that I want to make concerns (1) the degree of one's state of being informed, and (2) regardless of one's degree of knowledge, what does s/he know, or not, that will impact his/her greater understanding of the text in question. Or, as we shall see later on in my viewing of the films included in this book, the potentiality of signification of the text/ film in question. These two attributes — the viewer's greater understanding of the film watched and the significability of said film — will afford us some intriguing observations and conclusions as we discuss the four films herein and their potential *inter*-action with their spectators. Indeed, as Panofsky states, "[w]hether we like it or not, it is the movies that mold, more than any other single force, the opinions, the taste, the language, the dress, the behavior, and even

---

[11] Zavala offers a third type of viewer in his keenly concise study, the "espectador cinéfilo," whose experience "es una de las más complejas en la cultura contemporánea. Cada espectador, a partir de su experiencia personal, tiene expectativas particulares ante cada nueva película. Las propuestas teóricas de la estética de la recepción cinematográfica permiten estudiar las características de cada experiencia particular" (73; ... is one of the most complex in contemporary culture. Each viewer, from his personal experience, has particular expectations before each new movie. The theoretical propositions of the aesthetics of cinematographic reception allow one to study the characteristics of each particular experience).

the physical appearance of a public comprising more than 60 per cent of the population of the earth" (94).

∅

A text is a text is a text, some might say — indeed, many within the world of interpretation theory might agree most likely to a qualified 'some extent.' Nonetheless, we would be naïve, to say the least, were we not to recognize that there are differences in texts that impact the interpreter in distinctive if not divergent and possibly contrasting ways. In an analogous fashion, we might say that within the world of semiotics, a sign is a sign with all of its peculiarities. Hence, this notion of a seemingly apparent similarity between texts and/or signs of diverse characteristics (e.g., written, filmic, figurative) coupled with the notion that each medium does indeed have its narratological diversity underscores my decision to resort to semiotics and other theoretical / methodological practices that are not specific to one medium or the other. This is also the reason why I decided to use the character Marcovaldo; he is a protagonist of a written text ("The Wrong Stop") in the role of a movie viewer / spectator, and we witness his acts of interpretation both within and outside the movie theater. It is a coupling of disparate media that are treated in a similar decodifying manner.

Another factor harmonious to the melding of the written and the filmic as 'text' is the fact that no two individuals are inextricably alike. We each have our own divergent cognitive position in the world, always discordant to some degree with that of others. This thus means that our sense of and involvement within the world of phenomena that surround us will be different from others. In the end, then, we can only admit that our own interpretation of signs will be at variance with, if not incongruous to, how others will interpret those same signs. The difference might be minimal, on the one hand; on the other, it might also be significant. The upshot, in the end, is that it will be different; no two interpretations are the same.

As we move from one film to the other in what follows, we will engage in a series of semiotic acts that will invest the various signs along the way with what I shall argue are our more convincing acts of interpretation. In our discussions of food, identity, language, and the sort, we shall also come to the realization that the more 'informed' the viewer, the greater the potentiality of signification of the text in question. Indeed, not only shall we underscore the privilege of the 'informed spectator,' but we shall, for sure, identify the 'informed Italian/American spectator,' since, as we stated above, no two individuals will interpret the same sign in the same way, for which, the greater one's cognitive awareness of and familiarization with the Italian/American phenomena that surround her/him, the more probable it is that this individual distinguishes him/herself from the greater profile that we know as the 'informed spectator/reader.'

WORKS CITED

Arnheim, Rudolf. 1982. *The Power of the Center: A Study of Composition in the Visual Arts.* Berkeley, CA: U California P, 1982.

_____. 1955. *Film as Art* (Berkeley: University of California Press): contains the contents of his earlier book in English *Film.* 1933. Trans., L. M. Sieveking and Ian F. D. Morrow. London: Faber and Faber.

_____. 1954. *Art and Visual Perception: A Psychology of the Creative Eye.* Berkeley, CA: U California P, 1954.

Benamou, Michel. 1976. "Foreword," Film: Interdisciplinary Approaches to Theory and Teaching: Part One. *Quarterly Review of Film Studies* 1.3: 7-9.

Berstein, Richard. 1983. *Beyond Objectivism and Relativism: Science, Hermeneutics, and Praxis.* Philadelphia: U of Pennsylvania P.

Bondanella, Peter. 2009. *A History of Italian Cinema.* New York: Continuum.

Calabretta-Sajder, Ryan. 2017. "Beyond the 'Male Gaze': Conceiving the 'Fourth' Gaze in *La bestia nel cuore*" in *Writing and Performing Female Identity in Italian Cinema.* Virginia Picchietti and Laura Salsini, eds. New York: Palgrave. 105-124.

Calvino, Italo. 1963. *Marcovaldo, ovvero le stagioni in città*, with illustrations by Sergio Tofano (Turin: Einaudi. In English, *Marcovaldo: Or the Seasons in the City*, tr. William Weaver. New York: Harcourt Brace Jovanovich, 1983.

Dondis, Donis A. 1973. *Primer of Visual Literacy*. Cambridge, MA: MIT Press.

Feyerabend, Paul. 1975. *Against Method: Outline of an Anarchistic Theory of Knowledge*. London: New Left Books.

Foucault, Michel. 1979. *Discipline and Punish: The Birth of the Prison*. New York: Vintage Books; originally published as *Surveiller et punir: Naissance de la prison*. Paris: Bibliothèque des Histoires, 1975.

_____. 1973. *The Birth of the Clinic: An Archaeology of Medical Perception*. New York: Pantheon; originally published as *Naissance de la clinique: une archéologie du regard médical*. Paris: Presses Universitaires de France, 1963.

Gadamer, Hans-Georg. 1988. *Truth and Method*. New York: The Crossroad Publishing Company.

Geertz, Clifford. 1979. "From the Native's Point of View: On the Nature of Anthropological Understanding" in *Interpretive Social Science: A Reader*. Paul Rabinow and William M. Sullivan, eds. Berkeley: University of California Press.

Iser, Wolfgang. 1980. *The Act of Reading: A Theory of Aesthetic Response*. Baltimore: Johns Hopkins University Press.

Mulvey, Laura. 1975. "Visual Pleasure and Narrative Cinema," *Screen* 16.3 (Autumn): 6-18.

Panofsky, Erwin. 1995 (1936). "Style and Medium in the Motion Pictures" in *Three Essays on Style*. Irving Lavin, ed. Cambridge, MA: MIT Press. 91-128

_____. 1972. *Studies in Iconology: Humanistic Themes in the Art of the Renaissance*. New York: Harper & Row. 5–9.

_____. 1955. *Meaning in the Visual Arts*. Garden City, NY: Doubleday.

Peirce, Charles Sanders. 1931-1935. *The Collected Papers of Charles Sanders Peirce*. Vols. I-VI Charles Hartshorne and Paul Weiss, eds. Cambridge, MA: Harvard University Press.

Rees, A. L. and Frances Borzello, eds. 1988. *The New Art History*. Atlantic Highlands, NJ: Humanities International P.

Sartre, Jean Paul. 1993. *Being and Nothingness*. New York: Washington Square Press; originally published as *L'Être et le néant: Essai d'ontologie phénoménologique. Paris :* Èditions Gallimard, 1943.

Tamburri, Anthony Julian. 2017. "Il sistema di segni del cinema italiano/americano: code-switching e la significabilità di *Mean Streets* di Martin Scorsese," *Ácoma* (Fall-Winter): 108-121.

_____. 2015. "Viewing *Big Night* as Easy as One, Two, Three: A Peircean Notion of an Italian/American Identity." *Luci e ombre* 3.1 (Genn.-Mar): http://rivistalucieombre.com/sommario_ numero1_annoIII;

_____. 2003. *Re-reading: Guido Gozzano, Aldo Palazzeschi, and Italo Calvino*. Madison, NJ: Fairleigh Dickinson UP, 2003.

_____. 1994. "In (Re)cognition of the Italian/American Writer: Definitions and Categories." *Differentia, review of italian thought* 6/7 (Spring/Autumn 1994): 9-32;

_____. 1990. "Aldo Palazzeschi's *:riflessi*. Toward a Notion of a 'Retro-Lector'." *The American Journal of Semiotics*. 7.1-2 (1990): 105-24.

Turner, Victor. 1995 (1969). *The Ritual Process: Structure and Anti-Structure*. Chicago: Aldine Transaction.

van Gennep, Arnold. 1961 (1909). *The Rites of Passage*. Chicago: University of Chicago Press.

Zavala, Lauro. 1994. *Permanencia voluntaria. El cine y su espectador*. Xalapa, Ver.: Universidad Veracruzana, 1994.

Old World versus New. Or, Opposites Attract
Emanuele Crialese's *Nuovomondo*

"Voi siete il futuro nostro!"

The priest in Petralia Sottana,
saying goodbye to Rita and Rosa

The opening scenes of Emanuele Crialese's *Nuovomondo* set the stage for an ever-developing series of contrasts that grow throughout the film. On the one hand, these contrasts are based on real differences between the characters' real-life situations and what they may or may not expect in the United States. On the other, said contrasts are based on non-realistic beliefs, such as the giant coins and vegetables that Salvatore and his family see in the postcards his American brother sends back to him and his family from the United States, having emigrated years before. In addition, we find our characters, as well, swimming in a river of milk with giant carrots floating around them.

ON THE HOME-FRONT

Our first introduction to Salvatore's Sicily is the mountainous terrain that opens the film. As such, it truly could not be more different than what Salvatore and family could expect in the United States. The viewer is introduced to Salvatore's world as a treacherously barren and rocky area of Sicily, apparently incapable, here at the outset, of offering up anything but the belief that things can get better, as Salvatore and his son Angelo climb in order to pay homage to and ask for help from the Virgin Mary, to whom a small simple shrine exists at the top of this dangerous, grey mountainside. Salvatore is basically in search of a sign that will confirm for him the rationale for his desire to follow his brother and therefore emigrate to the United States.

One of the more poignant characteristics of this opening scene is (1) what they are bringing, and (2) how they are dressed. For all

15

practical reasons, they are dressed in tattered shirts and pants, bare-foot, carrying rocks in their mouths; and from carrying the rocks in their mouths this distance, their lips are slightly bleeding. Also, equally incisive, is the very opening shot; we see a white rock, in the shape of what could be a mountain from afar, and suddenly a hand appears, and it is Salvatore's, climbing over the rock's edge and into our view, with a goodly sized rock in his bleeding mouth. All this clearly speaks to struggle and sacrifice, be they immediate and concrete, in these two men's struggle to climb this mountain and make their sacrifice of bringing the rock to the Madonna, be they metaphorical of the more long-term struggles and sacrifices of the homeland as well as what is to come. The scene, in other words, has the dual function of signifying (1), for the moment, the struggles our characters face on a daily basis in this seemingly God-forsaken land that seems incapable of feeding its people, and (2), long-term, analogous sacrifices these people will make on their journey to the United States, as well as their future lives there.

They never touch the rocks they carry in their mouths, before they deliver them. It seems they must bring them to the Madonna untouched by human hands, in order to preserve the purity of the sacrifice they are making. Tattered as they are, barefoot and cov-ered with dirt from their climb, they are eventually engulfed in a mist of fog/clouds as they climb higher, almost as if they were en-tering a sphere of the divine, open only to those mortals who are worthy because of their sacrifice. Such a distinction between the seemingly divine and the human is also underscored by another scene in which Crialese uses the camera in a most ingenious man-ner. As Salvatore and Angelo make this climb up a hazardous mountainside, at a certain point the camera pulls back to a wide shot of the entire hill, comprised primarily of light brown and grey rocks. At this point, the viewer can hardly make out the two figures as they climb the mountain. In the meantime, the camera pulls back even further, to a total birds-eye view of the mountainside, as the two men, in the end, are completely engulfed by the mountainside of light brown and gray, and a mist eventually begins to cover the landscape just before the film shifts to another scene.

SIGNS TAKEN TO WONDER

When Salvatore and Angelo finally make it to the top, to this most simple shrine consisting of a wooden cross made out of tree branches, they deposit the stones—literally dropping them from their mouths at the foot of the shrine—and ask for a sign as to whether they should stay or leave, promising not to leave until they get their response in the form of a sign of some sort. That sign does in fact materialize; it comes in the form of postcards from America. Salvatore's other son, Pietro, a seemingly mute young man, arrives with postcards sent from his American uncle. These postcards, we see, contain trumped up photos of unrealistic scenes that Salvatore interprets as a sign to depart for the United States: one shows a giant onion in a wheelbarrow, the other a tree that grows money, and a third a giant chicken.

The two men's climb to the top—their search for justification to leave for the new world—is soon juxtaposed to an old-world exorcism that Salvatore's mother Fortunata, a local healer, performs on a young woman who believes to be cursed, supposedly possessed by a snake in her belly. The two scenes—one clearly directed toward the new world, the other deeply rooted in the old—counter each other and form a neat pair of opposites. Such *coincidentia oppositorum* comes to the surface at this time in another form. When one of the two young women destined for America, Rosa, first brings to Salvatore's mother an envelop containing the above-mentioned postcards, she (Fortunata) responds: "No, no, io non mi fido a leggere parole di carta" ("No, no, I do not trust reading paper words"), to which the young woman retorts, "No, no, queste non sono parole di carta, queste sono cose vere" (But these are not paper words, these are real things."). They are, she eventually says, things from the "terra nuova" ("new land"). At this point, once Fortunata examines the postcards, she tells her grandson Pietro to burn them. Of course, he does not. This brief conversation that takes place between Fortunata and the young woman soon to leave for America is poignant in two ways. First, we witness a clash between old-world thinking and new-world adventurism. Fortunata is a "natural" healer steeped in the old-world ways of nature and superstition.[1] Her desire to remain so is manifested by her order to her grandson to burn the postcards, which would obviously eliminate any sign for Salvatore to depart for the new world—however exaggerated it may be here—in what we only can assume is her neatly systematized old-world philosophy. The "terra nuova" simply cannot coexist in the old world, not even in a represented form such as a photograph, however trumped up it may be.[2]

The second point here is extra-textual and, to a significant degree, rhetorically self-reflexive. In the very brief conversation between Fortunata and the young woman with the postcards, we see that words have no value in that Fortunata does not trust in them: "No, no, io non mi fido a leggere parole di carta." Instead, the young woman responds, these are not "parole di carta, queste sono cose vere." Namely, that which is represented by words is not trustworthy, the logos, we see at this point, does not possess any semiotic valence for Fortunata. Instead, that which does have a semiotic function for both the young woman and Fortunata are the pictures, the visual; "queste sono cose vere" because they belong to the realm of the visual. That which is ocular is thus perceptible and discernible, and consequently "real," whereas that which is verbal is not. The visual therefore trumps the logos in this scene.[3]

---

[1] Later in the film, when the entire family is on its way out of Sicily and must pass through what we assume is Palermo and its coincidental bureaucracy, a doctor wants to sell Salvatore a cure for Pietro's muteness. Fortunata, incredulous, intervenes saying that what the man is trying to pawn off is rubbish, for she knows all too well since she is a "medica," as she says, thus creating more semiotic elasticity in the signs we encounter in the film.

[2] For more on Fortunata's rejection of the "new world" from a linguistic point of view, see Lorena Carbonara (128).

[3] There are undoubtedly other reasons we might add to why Fortunata (as well as the others) may not trust "parole di carta." First, we know that Fortunata and her companions are illiterate. As such, it is most logical that they would not trust that which they cannot read/decipher. A second reason may very well be steeped in officialdom. Namely, the written for those in this time represents the State, the national government. And since the State's view of the South has been debatable since *illo tempore*, it is not too far-fetched to

The self-reflexive element is precisely this; Crialese tells his story through pictures, not with words. In so doing, he also manipulates the semiotic value of the images he employs. While they are all realistic to a certain degree, his manipulation of the combination of images is what stands out and, to an extent, is what is ever so implied at this early juncture in the film. It is as if, through this first young woman, he is informing his viewer of what is to come. Yet, through Fortunata's rejection also of the images that she is told are "cose vere," one might suspect Crialese is also warning his viewer that the apparent meaning of some signs s/he will encounter, especially at their face value, might be cast by the wayside.

Such a message that the visual may also be susceptible to skepticism comes to the fore when the second young woman, we are told, is cursed; she has a "serpent in her belly" ever since she found out Don Ercole had promised her and her friend to two rich men in the United States, someone whom they obviously do not know. In a certain sense, then, Fortunata herself underscores the possibility of semiotic skepticism in the visual when she performs the so-called exorcism to rid the young woman of her curse. After tying her up in an apparent x-format, Fortunata places her hand under the woman's dress and for a short time seems to struggle with something, only to pull out from under the woman's dress a black snake. All of this takes place inside, in a darkened room, and we never really get a good look at the details of the scene, including the snake. What then adds to the skeptical element is Fortunata's own reaction; both before she pulls out the snake and immediately afterwards, she has a smile on her face. It is, I would contend, the second smile that plants the seed of skepticism since the scene ends at this very moment. This, of course, leaves the viewer, first, to wonder what just took place, in the dark, and, second, to ask what, pray tell, might Fortunata's smile actually communicate, both to the young woman as well as to the viewer.

---

consider Forunata's skepticism toward all that smacks of State government as something untrustworthy.

THE CALM BEFORE THE STORM

When Salvatore, his family, and the two young future brides destined to marry in the States leave their village, the scene is one of a daunting calm that is accompanied by an ominous sky; the sky is in fact an overcast, menacing blue that threatens some sort of a storm, and when juxtaposed to the rocky, barren land, as the horizon is, the viewer might readily presume a negative sequence. More than anything, it is the unknown that seems to weigh significantly in this scene. The faces of the travelers imply bewilderment if not fear, precisely because what they have to confront is yet to be encountered.

As before, here, too, we find the convergence of opposites. When Salvatore, his family, and the two betrothed leave their village of Petralia Sottana, they make their way to the city where they must now negotiate the administrative bureaucracy in order to emigrate. What stands out, at first, is the combination of an over-crowded market square with its coincidental cacophony. We see that the family is quite literally overwhelmed by this quasi city environment, compared to the calmer village life they knew so well. Hectic and crowded, Salvatore is clearly taken aback, unfamiliar so he seems with such an environment. His wish is clearly to get away from the crowd. Hence, the clash of two modes of living, one the calm mountain village, the other the hectic pace of the city marketplace.

What also stands out at this point in the film is their departure from their village. The camera's perspective is indeed intriguing. The shot is taken from the backs of a crowd, as those villagers who remain behind watch Salvatore and his traveling companions leave. At a certain point they exit the village, passing through a small entry way/ exit in a stone wall, and all we see is the carriage on the other side of the wall, a clear separation at this point early in the film. High up on the cart, looking back, is Salvatore as the cart and its passengers now disappear behind an even higher stonewall. The die is cast, so it seems; there is no turning back. From this last scene of the high stone wall and three donkeys—a reminder of the country-side way of life—the scene shifts to another set of stones, this time dark, the cobblestone of the market square, which immediately transforms itself into the hectic place it is.[4]

The two stone surfaces that occupy at two distinct moments at this juncture in the film should not go unnoticed. In a certain sense, they represent a blank surface, a sort of *tabula rasa* on which the Mancusos have yet to write their story. As they leave the village, the *tabula rasa* is white, something that represents among many things innocence, but it is, I would submit, a double-edged sign, one that can signify virtuousness as well as gullibility, two characteristics that can prove harmful to the Mancusos.[5] This said, the *tabula rasa* that opens the market scene is, in fact, dark, almost black. As such, we are now in a different signifying realm. First, black can represent the visual experience of visible light not reaching the eye; metaphorically, then, the unknown. But black is also the color of authority and seriousness; and it is here that the Mancusos come into contact for the first time with a full-court bureaucracy and its many attendants.

At this point we find one of our non-realistic scenes, and it is, to be sure, comical in intent to a certain degree, and literally cartoonish. The Mancusos pose behind one of those classical cutouts; this one, however, is of an upper-class family that, behind the cardboard, Salvatore, Fortunata, Pietro, and Angelo nicely fill out. Oddly, this is where Lucy comes into full screen with the Mancusos, having had only a previous, indirect encounter with her. She calmly walks over to Salvatore's character on the cutout, slowly looks at him and then slowly once more turns toward the camera, as the picture is then taken. This, I would submit, sets up yet another series of opposites. On the one hand, we have a clear distinction between fiction and reality. The Mancusos, peasant-farmers that they are, pose in this cutout as an upper-crust family, something they truly are not. This

---

[4] Francesco Pellegrino offers an intriguingly keen reading of this scene (175). His overall reading of the film, further still, is set nicely against an historical background.

[5] Let us also keep in mind that while in most Western countries white is the color for brides, in the East, conversely, it is the color for mourning and funerals. Let us also remember that Sicily is in many ways that meeting point in the Mediterranean Basin where, in various ways, East meets West.

contrast is further underscored by Lucy's presence, a truly upper-crust woman, or so she seems, who now comes into direct contact with the Mancusos. What this ultimately does is place the illiterate peasant — Salvatore and family — literally shoulder to shoulder with the upper-class individual — Lucy — literate, English, and bi-lingual to boot! The opposites could not be more distinct.

THE PROCESS OF A JOURNEY

Nuovomondo is clearly about Italian *emigration*, with *immigration* set off, to some degree, into an extra-textual zone of the film. Indeed, this is precisely that which remains particular to this film — that it is about the journey *to* the United States, not, instead, the emigrants' quotidian experience *within* the United States; we only see them at Ellis Island and nowhere else beyond the fateful port of entry.

What we witness throughout the film is a developing process of the turn-of-the-twentieth-century emigrants' decision to leave their home country and the resultant expectations and anxieties as well as bewilderment, confusion, and wonder that accompany them. Such feelings are apparent from the film's opening, as we saw above: the anticipation of leaving, the sense of fear and bewilderment that seem to reign over the Mancusos and the two betrothed, as they left the village; and the sense of being overwhelmed at both the market place as well as the processing office in the un-named port city of their departure. All of this contributes to an aura of mystery and unknown that accompanies and, at the same time, assails our travelers.

In addition to the efficacious early scenes of the mountain climb, the fog, and the exorcism — all of which contributes to a sense of mystery, if not of a sur-reality, and thus places the narrative somewhere between the real and the surreal — another notably poignant and significant scene is that of the departure.[6] It all begins with the

---

[6] Margherita Heyer-Caput speaks to the notion of "hyperreality" in her 2013 essay (272). See also, Simonetta Milli Konewko's 2015 essay for notions of the fantastic and the realistic adopted by Crialese in *Nuovomondo*. In a third essay that also appeared after the initial publication of my essay is Teresa Fiore's 2017 "Realist and Magical Realist Emigration Voyages in Criaslese's *Nuovomondo*" in which she rehearses much of what I discuss here

camera panning a mass of individuals with the Mancusos taking up the end of a line. Pietro, taking up the rear of the family's line, walks with his head up as he turns around, looking in wide-eyed wonder, and yet he moves forward. The camera then concentrates on the mass of people sitting, obviously waiting their turn to board either this ship or another yet to arrive. Within the visual, we see the wheelers and dealers' last-minute efforts to sell their wares, be they the bogus remedies or the many trinkets that pay homage to the various saints.

At this point there is a most effective transition. The scene shifts immediately to the boarding process, as the camera shot from above quickly shows the end of what we might readily assume is the upper class's boarding. The camera then widens its field, and we hear a voice calling for the "terza classe" (third class) to board. As the camera takes into its view from yet higher above the large crowd of third-class passengers, we witness a literal mob of people pushing and shoving each other in their negotiation to board. In the middle of this crowd, we find the Mancusos, as they occupy center screen and make it to the gangplank. Two thoughts come to mind at this moment for the viewer. First, we see Salvatore once more engulfed by and within an overwhelming mass; before it was the inanimate mountainside of his home village, this time it is the animate mass of other emigrants leaving for the same purpose, to find a better life in the United States. In the first instance, at that time, he literally and metaphorically rose to the top of the mountain. Here, he also rises to the top, this time of the gangplank, literally.[7] In order to do so, he, with the other travelers in third class, must enter into the belly of the ship, as we spectators now witness how each individual disappears through the door of the ship. At this point, there is an intermittent scene with Pietro who, obviously fearful of

through the lens of transnationalism: "…Crialese has fundamentally crafted a transnational film in which the figurative condensation of the diaspora in the microcosm of the transoceanic ship allows him to address the peculiar transnational formation of a country of regions like Italy within a dynamic framework of demographic movements" (40). Finally, Anita Virga discusses this contrast on two occasions: as "modi realistiti… per essere contraddetti" (2015, 73-75) to the slightly modified formula of "reality vs. representation" (2018, 56).

[7] As we shall see later, he also rises to the top in yet another manner, namely metaphorically.

the unknown behind the door as he gazes up at the strange, enormous structure of a ship he is supposed to enter, turns back in an
attempt to run back down the gangplank, only to be pulled back up
by his father.

These two actions may each take on obvious secondary meanings. Indeed, the crossing of that threshold into the ship's under-
belly may readily reference the notion of the immigrant's disap-
pearance from his home country. His prolonged absence from his
paese will effect a sort of memory loss on the part of the home-
town collective consciousness, and thus the immigrant *qua* Italian
eventually ceases to exist. This potential status of the immigrant
clearly directs him into an interstitial place, that world of liminality
where ambiguity, indeterminacy, and, on the positive side, open-
ness may reign.[8] Or, as may have been the case with immigration,
any clear sense of identity falls by the wayside, resulting in a potential socio-psychological, if not also cultural, state of bewilderment. This combined onslaught of removal (read, being forgotten)
and uncertainty (read, liminality), in turn, thus provokes Pietro to
turn away from the ocean liner, now that preeminent sign of identity nullification.

At this juncture, we encounter one of the most effective scenes
in the film, the ship's actual departure from the dock. From yet another birds-eye view, we see nothing but people occupying the entire screen. Most of them are of one size, the others a bit smaller.
The larger sized group of people are moving, *en masse*, to the left,
accompanied by a quasi-ominous clanging and one or two other
boat sounds, the people, instead, both on the ship and on shore remain silent. As the ship draws away from the dock, the clanging
continues at its normal beat while the engine's pistons seem to have
picked up their speed. With everyone still quiet, and the water between the ship and the dock clearly signaling the separation of the
one group from the other, and therefore from the homeland, the
two crowds of people stare at each other, as the gap grows ever

---

[8] I am, of course, bouncing off of Victor Turner's notion of the liminal (1969/1995), who, in
turn, is bouncing off of Arnold van Gennep (1909/1961).

larger. The scene suddenly shifts to the people on board as the ship's whistle blows loudly. All the passengers suddenly look upward toward the camera, a few covering their ears, still silent. The camera continues to span the deck, and thus the passengers, still and quiet as they stand looking upward, for another sixteen seconds, until the scene quickly changes to the third-class cabin, now a most hectic and, literally, dark experience in the belly of the ship.

But before this shift in scenes takes place, our traveling companions are once again at center screen. This time, however, only the three younger women appear, as the two betrothed flank Lucy — "la rossa," as the bureaucrat called her back on shore — who now wears red gloves on her folded hands, which immediately grab the viewer's gaze as they contrast against a backdrop of blues, and grays, and black. Why these three stand out clearly leads to further speculation as to their possible semiotic functions. As women they, more than the men, represent a creative and thus perpetuating function of the Italian immigrant in the States. Are they the future of this emigration? Do they represent those who will eventually succeed on this trip? These are some of the questions that come to mind at this time; and in retrospect, it will become clear that their particular functions in the greater scheme of things in this small world of the Mancusos, Rita, Rosa, and Lucy are. Their "intentio operis," we shall see, will come to the surface and impact, as is customary, on our own "intentio lectoris" as viewers of the film.[9]

Once the travelers move below to settle themselves into their transoceanic living conditions, we observe them settling into the third-class cabin. During this process, we witness the crowded conditions of third-class travel — or better, steerage; we come to learn of the various towns from which the emigrants hail. The illiteracy of the many is underscored at one point; and, quite keenly, we learn that Salvatore's universe was, up to this point, limited only to Petralia Sottana, as he wonders how he is going to cope on

---

[9] Of course, our "intentio lectoris" will come to the fore, since we can never really know the "intentio auctoris" of a text, though we might connote an "intentio operis." For more on all three concepts, see Umberto Eco (1988, 147-68).

this trip sleeping with all these "stranieri" (foreigners). In fact, at this point, we witness Salvatore's full-blown innocence in his knowledge, or lack thereof, of the world outside his small village. This innocence manifests itself in a number of ways. First, the above-mentioned reference he makes about all these "stranieri," to which his fellow traveler, Nicola Esposito, responds:

> NICOLA: Stranieri? Ma dove sono tutti questi stranieri? Qua siamo tutti italiani.
> SALVATORE: Italiani?
> NICOLA: Italiani.

> NICOLA: Foreigners? But where are these foreigners? Here we're all Italians.
> SALVATORE: Italians?
> NICOLA: Italians

Then, there is his questioning of language and what language they are all speaking.

> SALVATORE: E se ci son quale lingua parlano?
> NICOLA: Perché lei non lo sa che è italiano?
> SALVATORE: Se lo dici tu.

> SALVATORE: And if there are what language are they speaking?
> NICOLA: Why, you don't know it's Italian?
> SALVATORE: If you say so."

While on the one hand Salvatore has proven to be most adventurous, since it is indeed his desire and ultimately his decision to move his family to the United States, his limited experience with and/or knowledge of the outside world is, to some degree, astounding. And it is manifested here, linguistically as well, when we see the multiple definitions of the adjective "straniero" at play: "stranieri" as those of another local village, though within those geo-political confines we know as Italy, versus those of a different nationally sovereignty, for instance. Then, of course, one might read "italiano" as the moniker for the common language of the group on the ship, regardless of particular regional inflections and accents.[10] One of these particularities, for sure, might be considered the different pronouns Salvatore and Nicola use. To Salvatore's question of what language is everyone speaking, Nicola responds with the formal "lei", whereas Salvatore, in reacting with the proverbial "if you say so" in Italian, uses the "tu." Such a distinction in this situation can only demonstrate the difference in social and cultural exposure of the two gentlemen at hand. Salvatore is truly the innocent and/or naive immigrant who, if things were to become problematic, might very well end up victim to a series of scams and misfortunes.

Finally, and still within the realm of language, we witness, in an etymological sense, the confusion of oral language. Salvatore asks Nicola, his more informed traveling companion, when will they see "'sto grande Luciano" ("this Big Luciano"), to which a third person responds, "no, certo vuol dire l'oceano, il grande oceano" ("no, he must mean the ocean, the big ocean"). This seemingly fleeting though moving episode is, to be sure, one of the more significant communication acts in which Crialese engages. He underscores, on the one hand, the absolute lack of worldly knowledge that existed among some of these emigrants; they could not distinguish between the aural sounds of "grande Luciano" and "grande oceano" (or, perhaps, "grande l'oceano"). One reason, of course, is their language and the difference in pronunciation between dialect and standard Italian, for which the dialect pronunciation of "l'oceano" is misunderstood for the masculine name "Luciano." On the other hand, this episode points to a rhetorically self-reflexive element, that of the polysemic characteristic of language for which one sign ("l'oceano") is taken for another ("Luciano"). Language, we come to understand more convincingly from this exchange, grounds us; thus to rephrase Descartes's proverbial motto of "Cogito, ergo

---

[10] Of course, one might also want to see "italiano" as a noun/adjective describing any language — dialect or standard — these travelers speak to each other. Such a categorization obviously universalizes the notion of "dialect" and, in so doing, also enhances its sociolinguistic "value," as we might say.

sum," we may know utter "Loquor, ergo sum," an obvious rule of thumb for this aspect of language in *Nuovomondo*.[11] But language, as we saw earlier in the film, when Fortunata tells Rosa that she does not trust in "leggere parole di carta," is clearly in strict competition with, if not secondary to, the visual.

Literacy versus illiteracy continues; the first example is when the women take their quarters, and one peasant woman lays claim on what is Lucy's bed. When Lucy explains that it is indeed hers, and she shows the peasant woman her receipt for that bed, Rosa is momentarily befuddled, but she does acquiesce, perhaps even a bit miffed, stating she does not know how to read, as we witness:

> LUCY: Scusi, signora, questo è il mio letto.
> ROSA: No, qui ci sto io.
> LUCY: Vede, è scritto qui.
> ROSA: Non lo sacci' a leggere io.

> LUCY: Excuse me, Madam, this is my bed."
> ROSA: No, I'm here.
> LUCY: Look, it's written here.
> ROSA: I don't know how to read.

This admission of illiteracy, we might assume, is her apology for the mix-up. But it is also indicative of, once again, the skepticism for language and all that it represents: indeterminacy, ambiguity, and uncertainty, on the one hand, and officialdom and thus power, on the other; neither of which, as we saw before, subtends any genuine notion of reality. It is no casual coincidence, we must then admit, that this latest incident with Lucy includes Rosa; it was in fact Rosa who first brought the postcards to Fortunata, underscoring at that early juncture in the film that what was represented in those postcards were indeed "cose vere" as opposed to the unreliably representative "parole di carta."

---

[11] All of this manipulation of language, we must recognize, is done by Crialese with the utmost respect and sensitivity with regard to Salvatore and his traveling companions.

THE JOURNEY: A SEMIOTIC TALE

The journey across the ocean is steeped to a significant degree in gender and class. Once the ship has finally set sail and the passengers first appear on deck, the initial scene has Lucy leaning over the side rail. As she lifts her head and looks in one direction, we find the well-heeled Don Luigi and two friends, all finely dressed, as they greet her in the most gentlemanly of ways. Lucy then turns away to look in the other direction, where Salvatore and his two sons, caught staring at her, immediately look away. At this moment, we also witness a quasi cat-and-mouse game; the three peasant men slowly shift their gaze back at her only to find her smiling at them, mouthing a cheerful "Buon giorno."

This scene might surely have another semiotic function, indeed double, at the very least. Lucy, we see, is literally caught in the middle of two men, Don Luigi on the one hand and Salvatore on the other. As such she is literally caught in the middle of two "courtiers," or so it seems. Such *in-between-ness* is not uncharacteristic of the physical journey as one end point and gender as the other. Lucy seemingly remains the love interest of both men, though Don Luigi also embraces the role of a matchmaker, to put it nicely, as he introduces Lucy at one point to another well-heeled gentleman, Signor Belvedere, "the largest purveyor of ice in New York City." Such *in-between-ness*, we might submit, also allows her a certain privilege, as she does find herself in the position of being able to choose, however difficult this may be for her.[12]

This double-sided journey of the physical and the gendered is also accompanied by a third component, class, insofar as we also witness a socio-economic journey based in clear class difference; the distinction could be no clearer than the comparison of the three well-heeled gentlemen on the one end, and Salvatore and his two sons on the other, these last three dressed in tattered clothes. That said, we now have a triangle of sorts, three possible reference points for which Lucy is the center. Lucy becomes a Peircean sign insofar as she possesses the capability of multiple meanings on multiple

---

[12] The notion of *in-between-ness* undergirds Heyer-Caput's essay.

levels. But she is a Peircean sign that also resembles a semiotic knot, since the multiple meanings also have the potential of canceling each other out.[13] She is, in a sense, all *and* nothing within this semiotic process, shifting evermore for the reader in her signifying functionality in the film. It is indeed her sense of *nothingness* that subtends her *all-ness*.[14] Lucy is thus gender, class, and journey; she is the all-encompassing sign that anchors, to a significant (pun intended) degree, the various signs that constitute the film's apparent semiotic web, its potential communiqué. In her above-men-tioned position of centrality—an analogue, for sure, to her liminality—Lucy thus serves as that ultimate lynchpin that ties together the various aspects of the emigration and/or immigration experience at the beginning of the twentieth century, from the general to the specific (i.e., from the physical to the ideological).

The actual physicality of the trip is manifested in a variety of ways in the movie. We already saw the departure from their home village and the clash of cultures once they arrived in the city. We also saw how they were treated leaving that city (with the exploiting sellers of wares and snake oils, for lack of another term). We also witnessed how the third-class passengers, especially, huddled in groups on the dock, as if corralled by a dominating force. These are some of the physical and mental challenges the emigrants had

---

[13] I have in mind Floyd Merrell's notion of "one, two, three and back again" (2003, 33-51).

[14] As I have said elsewhere (1994, 255-73 and 2007a), in speaking of Palazzeschi's Perelà and empty centers in Palazzeschi's poetry and de Chirico's early paintings, "questo *nulla* che occupa i centri dei loro testi si presenta come una specie di combinazione di segni che sono autonomi e, per di più, slegati da qualsiasi referenzialità concreta. Essi poi costituiscono in termini peirceiani una "libertà illimitata", un *nulla* (dal latino *ne* + *ullus* [*non alcuno*]), che, ciononostante, continua a significare; esso significa *nessuna* (dal latino *ne* + *ipse* + *unus*) cosa. *Nulla* è la potenzialità illimitata per la generazione illimitata di *alcuna cosa*, ovvero *non una cosa stessa* (*ne* + *ipsa* + *una*)—cioè, il significato, il valore semantico, l'interpretazione, la quale è vera, per il lettore, solo in quanto essa sia 'semioticamente reale' (Merrell, 1991: 198)" (Tamburri, 2007a: 43-4; "this *nothing* that occupies the center of their texts figures as a sort of combination of signs that are autonomous and, furthermore, free from any concrete referentiality. They thus constitute in Peircean terms an "unlimited freedom," a *nothing* [from the Latin *ne* + *ullus* (*not any*)] that nevertheless continues to signify; it signifies not any [from Latino *ne* + *ipse* + *unus*] thing. *Nothing* is thus the unlimited potentiality for an unlimited generation of *some thing*; or, rather, *not one same thing* [*ne* + *ipsa* + *una*]—that is, the meaning [i.e., *interpretant*], the semantic value, the interpretation, which is true, for the reader, only insofar that it is 'semiotically real' [Merrell, 1991: 198]"; my translation).

to face. Yet, perhaps, one of the few most poignant episodes of the journey is the storm. It is here that the dangerous, life-threatening and life-altering aspects of emigration are reified in a series of scenes in which the third-class passengers are tossed about until they are left unconscious. This part of the storm is most efficaciously rendered by the constant changing of speed and light; at times we have regular motion and darkness, while other times the scene is slowed down, and the light disappears and vice versa.

The immediate results of the storm on the third-class passengers also manifest themselves shipside. At first, a series of individuals slowly comes into view on a deck scattered with debris. One by one, each is either dragging or carrying an ill or, unbeknownst to us, dead person. One of the tragedies of these journeys is reified through the young woman carrying what we soon realize is a dead infant. Wandering aimlessly, she first gives the child to Lucy, whose facial expression signals the child's fate. Taking back the child, the mother aimlessly wanders again, this time toward the ship's rail where, knowing full well that she could not keep her dead infant on board, buries the baby at sea as she drops the baby overboard and faints to the floor. Just before she drops the baby, there is in the background against the cloudy sky a sprouting sun, which is blocked by the mother figure, thus blackening her and rendering the sunlight as nothing less than a halo. Such a woeful scene—as the mother, alone, has to bury her baby at sea—is couched in this *quasi* religious hue of the halo, diminishing to some extent, one might wish to presume, the tragic aspects of the journey.[15]

Such an assumption might be signaled by the scene that follows. The women of third-class are now sitting in a sort of chain, brushing out each other's hair, as if preparing for some event. As the camera spans them, we notice first one young woman with her head down, and then soon after, we see all in a row four women we know. From front to back, we see first the woman, emotionless, who had to bury her baby at sea, is having her hair brushed by For-

---

[15] One might see a diminution insofar as the halo recalls the religious, which, for Catholics, means that the baby's soul has ultimately gone home to God.

tunata, who, in turn is having her hair combed by Rita, and further in the back of this row, we find Lucy combing some other woman's hair. The four women in our sights all represent something of poignancy. The first, loss of a child, one of the most heart-breaking experiences of the journey; the second, courage and fortitude of the old world; the third, as the priest stated just before their departure from Petralia, the future;[16] the fourth, that all-encompassing sign that here, as we contextualize it, represents risk, bravery, and good fortune. Indeed, in Lucy's case, regardless of any mystery that might surround her (e.g., the villagers' supposition of who, if at all, her husband may have been), Lucy is a woman in a foreign country (Italy) who decides to emigrate on her own. This, on its own, further adds to the imminence of the migratory act.

LUCY AND SALVATORE: OPPOSITES ATTRACT

Complicated further by Lucy's seemingly independent stance, the gender issue is centered in her presence throughout the film, with Fortunata and the others playing supporting roles. As stated earlier, Lucy's independence and courage to embark on the trip alone underscore a unique, female attitude of the time.[17] Such resolution is underscored by her determination to align herself with the Mancusos, as they have, on the surface, nothing really in common. This was rendered visually early on when Salvatore and family posed in the above-mentioned cutouts. As stated then, one of the numerous opposites in that scene is, of course, in the binomial Lucy-Salvatore: she, an urbane, upper-class individual, literate, Eng-

---

[16] Let us not forget what the priest actually stated at their departure. First, he asked them all, both travelers as well as those remaining behind, to smile. Then, looking at the travelers, Rita especially, he stated: "Voi siete il nostro futuro!" Such a statement is pregnant with meaning and brings to the fore a series of pertinent questions that, only until recently, have been asked. First, why does it seem that Italy has forsaken its historical emigration and the progeny of those who left? What, if anything, might the Italy of today owe to those whose parents, grandparents, and great-grandparents of those who struggled both during and after the voyage? This is not the place for such a prolonged discussion, much still needs to be said. Nevertheless, I would refer the reader to an earlier essay of mine in which I have raised these issues (2007b, 247-64).

[17] One might see an analogue in the fictional character Umbertina, of Helen Barolini's novel, *Umbertina* (1979). Each woman represents a truly different, independent type of female for this time in history, at the end of the nineteenth / beginning of the twentieth century.

lish, and bilingual; he, illiterate, a peasant farmer, who speaks dialect and believes in the magic of his homeland.

Until this point in the film, just before they disembark onto Ellis Island, there are three poignant scenes between Lucy and Salvatore. The first is the above-mentioned scene of the family portrait and the cutouts. The second scene takes place on deck as they each walk in opposite directions, and continuously look and acknowledge each other, only to meet up, inevitably, as their movement naturally requires. The third scene takes place just before landing, where we might notice a shift in point of view, as Salvatore and Lucy have their most personal conversation.

Having seen Lucy take control of the situation early on, attaching herself to the Mancusos both in the photo as well as part of their traveling group, we see instead that Salvatore now is becoming bolder, to a significant degree. In this second scene, in fact, Salvatore takes notice of Lucy, as he peers out from behind one of the large exhaust vents and glances at her, obviously on the other side of the ship's deck, walking slowing, her movements slightly slowed down by the camera. She then disappears behind another large exhaust fan only to reappear, she now looking in Salvatore's direction. Their movements are then repeated until they actually cross in front of each other. In all, these two minutes then switch to one of the unrealistic scenes of the movie. As Salvatore has, in this second episode of a cat-and-mouse game, his final look at Lucy, he fades behind an even larger exhaust fan, all white, which becomes a momentary blank from which then emerges a hat, and we realize that we are viewing Salvatore coming to the surface in a sea of milk. As he looks around in awe, he is joined by Lucy. While smiling at each other, an enormous carrot floats by, and they, immediately, grab on to it and perch themselves as if it were some sort of a lifesaver. The camera withdraws, and the scene comes to an end.[18]

---

[18] That this scene may possess a phallic referentiality is without question. Indeed, one might even think back to the exorcism scene where Fortunata removes, or so it seems, a snake from Rita's belly, thereby removing the curse. The potential phallic recall for both scenes deserves its own venue, this not being the proper one.

As we take a second glance at this scene, we notice, first of all, that there is no talking between them. On the ship's deck, they only look and smile at each other, no words are exchanged. Of course, such a scene has its inter-textual recall, especially for the informed viewer of Italian cinema. One is immediately reminded of the famous scene in *Mimì metallurgico ferito nell'onore* (1972) when Mimì (Giancarlo Giannini) and Fiore (Mariangela Melato) engage in a conversation of facial expressions and hand movements only. Here, too, we have a very similar situation; throughout the walk on deck Lucy and Salvatore look at each other, slightly smile, but never speak; even when they eventually meet up, Salvatore simply tips his hat and smiles. In the end, here too the visual trumps the logos.

It is the third scene that marks a significant shift in the relationship between Lucy and Salvatore. Up to this point, one could have readily made the argument that she had the upper hand. We saw her *invade* their space during the cutout photo; we also witnessed how she attached herself to the Mancuso family. Clearly, this is not demurring behavior. Now, however, things seem to shift, even if ever so slightly.

While Lucy continues in making her courageous request of marriage to Salvatore, he, more assured by all means, responds immediately in the affirmative, asking when and how: "Ma certo, magari ora!" ("but sure, right now perhaps"). Lucy, in her honest and candid manner, as we have already seen in the past, underscores that she is not marrying him for love, but that she needs a man in order to enter the United States. Salvatore, in turn, as secure as before, responds in like fashion: "Amore, e se manco ci conoscemo! Queste cose, ci vuol tempo. È giusto, è giusto?" ("Love, and if we don't even know each other! These things, it takes time. True, True?"). Lucy responds with a half committing "sì" only to be followed by Salvatore's superstitious move of cutting a lock of Lucy's hair so that they do not lose each other — Accusì non ci perdemo" ("This way we won't lose each other"), he tells her. And when she responds that she does not in fact believe "in magic," Salvatore's assuredness comes to the fore, highlighted by his statement, "Col tempo ci insegno tutto cos'è" ("With time I'll teach you what it all is."). The scene in fact closes with a silent close-up of the two, as if they were to kiss, but do not, and Salvatore, momentarily, clearly seems to have the upper hand.[19]

From here on, their roles vis-à-vis each other alternate, as each will occupy an active role according to the circumstance at hand. When Lucy's name is not called during the role-call for those to marry, she comes forward to let the immigration officers know that she has been overlooked. Salvatore is as confident as one can be, but his illiteracy causes him to rely on Lucy, as she now explains to the officials why he did not fill out the requisite forms. In this new world, Salvatore, still the countryman who relies on practicality and common sense, now learns early on, that language and bureaucracy are two necessities he will have to confront. His initial reaction to the forms is that Lucy no longer wishes to marry him, as he, seemingly disgruntled and disappointed, asks. Lucy now takes the upper hand and tells the immigration officer that this is indeed her role within their relationship, that she deals with these types of issues, filling out forms and the like.

At this point, an intriguing thing takes place. Lucy's hat falls off, as she continues to fill out the forms. Two physical characteristics stand out; her red hair and her red gloves, each of which had occupied, even if ever so momentarily, the center in previous scenes. It is very much the color red that underscores what we can readily call difference; she is English, woman, bi-lingual, and, we assume, bi-cultural. It is thus not an exaggeration to claim that throughout the film Lucy represents, among various possibilities, difference from the old world, and hence the "new world." The color, in itself, visually contrasts with the darkness that seems to surround instead the Mancusos and all that they represent. This is where Lucy is truly and literally a lynchpin, as stated above. Her filing out the forms allows both her and Salvatore to enter the United States, now married, having therefore overcome the bureaucracy that would have otherwise kept them out. She thus holds that position of centrality mentioned earlier; her liminality affords her a certain privilege that

---

[19] See Heyer-Caput on Lucy being saved by Salvatore (272-73).

benefits her and all with whom she associates. Such liminality, I submit at this time, is underscored by Lucy accepting not the traditional flower but indeed Salvatore's old-world derby, so that old and new worlds now come together, as Lucy and Salvatore are now ready to embark on this new adventure in the new world.

Lucy's liminality *qua* a semiotic function of the bridge between two cultures is best exemplified during a brief, seemingly insignificant scene that precedes the one above; this is when the women are packing up their things from the bunk area. At one point the scene slows down, and a church-like music beings to play. The physical placing of the four women is, to be sure, most intriguing. Lucy is just about center screen, with Fortunata to her right (the viewer's left) and Rosa and Rita, facing each other but looking down, are to Lucy's left (the viewer's right). As the scene progresses, slightly in slow motion, Rosa and Rita remain in their original pose. Instead, Fortunata turns to her left as Lucy turns to her right. At one point the two women are facing each other and seem to nod, ever so slowly, in agreement. About what they might agree at this point, we do not know. But the scene, and the glance they share, is one of acquiescence and not disagreement; in examining further the scene, we see that the one half of each woman's face is out of the viewer's sight.[20] That said, were we then to move them closer to each other, we would end up with a most intriguing and, I would submit, signifying image; we would have one face composed of these two women, one from the "old" world, the other of the "new"; and in the background, ready to benefit from this new person, indeed this new *woman*, are Rita and Rosa, poised to move forward as best deemed fit. This is where Lucy's tri-part sign of gender, class, and journey all come together and, we can only assume, all ends well.

THE [NON]ARRIVAL

Earlier in this chapter I dedicated a section to the "process" of the journey. What is significant, as I pointed out above, is not so

---

[20] In his essay, Pellegrino also speaks to the resolution of acquiescence and agreement between Lucy and Fortunata (186).

much the journey per sè; rather, it is the experience of interaction with the "new" that the immigrants encounter: namely, the people they meet, the conversations they have, and the changes that are born from these and other new concurrences.

The last forty-plus minutes of the film are dedicated to the various physical and psychological examinations of the immigrants, as well as other procedures they must confront. The difference between how the men and women are treated is notable. Whereas the men are in a sort of chaotic atmosphere, the women find themselves in a more sensitive surrounding. But there are even here striking differences in cultures, in addition to Italy / America, also country / city. Fortunata, for example, is not used to certain medical check-ups and protests strongly.

There is also the issue of practicality, especially during the so-called intelligence exams when the immigrants are supposed to replace the differently shaped pieces of wood back into the large frame, so they eventually form a flat surface. Salvatore creates a mini lean-to and another structure that would serve any worker of land as was Salvatore in Petralia Sottana back in Sicily. His response, indeed, with the self-congratulatory smile indicates such satisfaction on his part. But more striking here is Lucy's experience with the so-called intelligence test. She, seeing it more as a table game, as she in fact states, asked a question of the examiner, and the following conversation follows:

> LUCY: May I ask, I thought you were looking for illnesses, and contagious diseases?
> STATE EXAMINER: Unfortunately, Ma'am, it has been scientifically proven that lack of intelligence is genetically inherited, and it's contagious, in a way. We are trying to prevent below-average people from mixing with our citizens.
> LUCY: What a modern vision?

What today would be considered shocking was clearly acceptable for the turn-of-the-century scientific community. Furthermore, in Italy itself there were the likes of Cesare Lombroso and his notion of biological determinism — there was an archetype of an Italian "southern type race" as opposed to a "northern race" (1902) — not much different from what the state examiner implies in his statement to Lucy. And in yet a similar fashion, the notion of miscegenation, or something similar, was also highly discredited. In fact, during the above-mentioned, medical examination of the females, one of the American nurses says to Lucy that "[i]t is highly unlikely for an English woman to be traveling with Italians, you'll be questioned about that."[21]

This is the "new world," as it is often called herein. To be sure, the question of "old" world versus "new" world and what these two represent is underscored at this juncture when Fortunata, now called up to the table for her intelligence exam, tells the Ellis Island examiner that she is fine where she is sitting. The truly poignant aspect to this scene is when she questions the examiner with "Che volete da noialtri?" ("What do you want from us?"), to which he asks "Them who?" And she affectively underscores: "Tutta questa gente che è venuta dal vecchio mondo," as she clearly sees herself as part of a world that is different precisely because it is the "old world." This *coincidentia oppositorum* is subsequently solidified by the examiner himself when he states that they want to be sure that "they are fit enough to enter the *new* world" (emphasis added); and as the conversation continues, the couplet "new world" is repeated a couple of times.

These are some of the unpleasant concurrences these immigrants had to confront. Humiliation and denigration were willy-nilly part of the system. This carried over into the formal recognition of the so-called marriage arrangements. It is here that the women, especially, must undergo a process of anxiety, stress, and, as is demonstrated herein, disappointment, precisely because (1) they are literally on display, and (2) they are finally to meet for the first time the men to whom they were betrothed. Indeed, as both

---

[21] Ethnic difference and the fact that such difference was already present back in the colonial period has been nicely rehearsed by Stephen Steinberg in his classic study *The Ethnic Myth* (1981/1989).

the men in waiting and the newly arrived women take their places, the women are virtually on display; there is a most poignant camera shot, in fact, from the perspective of the men, as the camera is behind the men, with us seeing only the tops of some of their heads, yet on full display, facing us, are the women, many of whom are looking down. This initial introduction of the women *en masse*, and in this seemingly demurring position can potentially signify (1) the men's opinion of them, as it is their visual perspective that we as viewers share here, and/or (2) their future position in their respective marriages.

In addition to Ellis Island's recognition of Lucy and Salvatore as a betrothed couple, we witness others as well. As the camera pans up close the faces of the women especially, one cannot help but recognize such trepidation. Rita, for one, cannot even look up into her future husband's eyes; she remains with her head and eyes bent toward the floor, even as she sits. The opposite, instead, at least at the outset, is what we find in Rosa's reaction. She lashes out, calling him a wretched, ugly liar, she now finding him older and shorter than she was made to believe. With this outburst, she may very well have lay the groundwork for the relationship, we will never be sure. For she surely did not have to leave Italy for this; after all, as she states, she has a father there. Then there is the case of Delores Torres, the Spanish women notably older than the others, who had been promised to someone. He, unfortunately for her, had yet to identify himself, and she was left to wait for him for days at Ellis Island.[22]

$\wp$

---

[22] Like very few seemingly secondary scenes in *Nuovomondo*, this one is undoubtedly one of the more poignant. While we saw that the norm was for young women to be sent to the United States to marry significantly older men, in this case the situation is the opposite. Delores Torres is clearly older than the other women who surround her; and the camera indeed reminds us of this, as it places her in the middle of a group of younger women. Second, once she pleads for her mysterious betrothed to identify himself, a notably younger man slowly rises, carefully uncovering his young face to her view. The camera then switches back to Delores, only to show her disconcerted state of mind and obvious realization that this marriage was not going to take place. All of this, we need remember, takes place immediately after Rosa lashes out at her betrothed, accusing him of lying about his age.

As the title of this section indicates, we never witness the arrival of the immigrants onto what we might call *terra firma*; at film's end, for instance, we leave them at Ellis Island. Most of the immigrants, from our perspective as viewers of the film that is, never truly see America. When, for instance, they are still on the ship as it draws near, the fog is too thick for them to see the shore. In addition, once it seems they have passed through the process of exams and the like, the men find themselves in a room with high windows of frosted glass. In order to see New York, for instance, the men need to climb up to the top of the window where the glass is clear; and as far as we viewers can ever know, only these three enjoy the privilege of actually seeing the "new world."[23]

Also, as we saw before in Crialese's *ars rhetorica*, here too he offers his viewer an iconic scene of these three men, now shadows against a lighted window, as it recalls a classical Italian painting of sorts, a triptych of three men, as if produced not at the beginning of the twentieth century but instead in the Middle Ages if not during the Renaissance. This, too, we might contend, is yet another form of *coincidentia oppositorum* where the old world is set fully against the new, and the men, in this instance, find themselves in between, in that liminal space of migrants still in search of a prefix that is either "e" or "im."[24]

At this same time and in another episode of the film, the dichotomy "old world / new world" comes to the fore and is now set aside yet another binomial of opposing terms, "older generation / younger generation." We find Fortunata and Pietro sitting side by side, silent and seemingly incommunicative when Pietro, looking at his grandmother, all of a sudden, grabs her face and shakes his head in disapproval. She, instead, nods ever so slightly in the affirmative and then looks away. There is a sudden shift to an-

---

[23] With regard to "fog" and its semiotic influence, I remind the reader of Marcovaldo's moviegoing experience in the story, "The Wrong Stop," that I referenced in my introduction.

[24] From a Peircean perspective of "unlimited semiosis," as Umberto Eco labeled the process (1976, 71-74), one might readily perceive in this image a topsy-turvy Mount Calvary reference insofar as, while Mount Calvary references the crucifixion and hence killing of Christ, this is a positive and therefore it transforms itself into an upside-down referent. In turn, for a more conventional reading of this episode, see Michaud (54).

other scene in which we have the entire Mancuso family full screen: Fortunata, the old-world matriarch, is center screen surrounded by her son and two grandsons. It is at this point that the administration of Ellis Island—namely, the United States—"plays God," as Fortunata had implied earlier. They tell Salvatore that his mother is too feeble-minded and his son mute, two characteristics that, according to United States policy, repatriate immigrants back to their homeland.

Salvatore's response harks back to an old-world practicality, one that provokes him to ask a series of questions and then offer a basic, logical solution. For with all this land and all this work, how can you keep people out? And if his son cannot speak, better for all; he will not bore anyone, nor can he complain about matters. Finally, as to his mother, if she speaks too much, as they claim, he will then keep her inside. These are simple, practical solutions, according to Salvatore, to problems that he obviously does not see as problems.[25] Such old-world practicality was already on display during his intelligence exam with the pieces of word and the frame within which he had to place them; as we saw, instead of laying them flat, he built small lean-tos.

If Fortunata was indeed an excessive talker, and Pietro were in fact the mute we all thought he was, this couplet of grandmother and grandson now comes to a signifying head, and we now see how they had indeed been inextricably tied. Through a good deal of the first half of the trip, Fortunata had surely been talkative and opinionated, we might say. However, as the trip progressed, she seemed to grow more silent; indeed, a good number of the immigrants were silent.

Fortunata's silence toward the end of this trip, however, does not, strangely enough, impede her from communicating with her grandson Pietro; which is precisely what takes place minutes be-

---

[25] It is curious indeed how Salvatore equates "debole di mente" (feeble-minded) to speaking too much, whereas the Ellis Island officials might have seen it as a sign of a disorder, as it was sometimes characterized. Excessive acts, especially if a social act, were seen as possible symptoms of feeble-mindedness. See, for example: Henry Herbert Goddard (1914); and Edgar A. Doll (1917).

fore this final scene of the family together. And it is here that the "older generation / younger generation" opposition is played out to its entirety. Fortunata is now mute, communicating with her son and grandsons only via her facial expressions. And after Salvatore makes his final pitch to have both his mother and son remain in the States, it is his son, Pietro, the mute, and not his mother, who verbally articulates her desire to return to Italy, and that they, instead, should remain in the States:

> Papà, la nonna mi disse che vuole morire a casa. E mi disse pure che noialtri dobbiamo stare accà.

> Pa, grandma told me she wants to die at home. And she also told me that we should stay here.

As Pietro makes these two statements, divided by a few seconds of silence, Fortunata first caresses Salvatore's face with her hands, then she passes to Angelo, equally affectionate, only to end with a caress accompanied by a long, smiling stare into Pietro eyes.

The final scene is of all four, with Fortunata still in the middle, both Salvatore and Angelo looking into the camera, and Fortunata and Pietro looking down. This scene then dissolves into the ever-mythical river of milk, in which we now find not just the Mancuso family but, in fact, many of the immigrants who traveled with them.

The combination of Pietro's two statements and other actions at this point stand to be some of the more poignant moments in this film from the point of view of opposites: namely, old world / new world and old generation / new generation. Fortunata is old world, and of the older generation; with her grandson she forms half of the binomial that underscores a *coincidentia oppositorum* that is, we now realize, doubly layered. It is a duality that is at once horizontal (from one world to the other) and vertical (i.e., chronological, from elder to younger). This new world, at this juncture, has truly had an impact on the two members of this couplet. Fortunata, old world, cannot stay in the new world; she urges to return, in order to "morire a casa," with "casa" being in many ways an operative word. For this process of the journey, as well as the initial encounter with the new world, proves to be antithetical to her being; she simply does not see herself in this new space. Pietro, on the other hand, experiences a metamorphosis that is both spiritual as well as physical; especially when we think back to the scene of embarkation when he wanted to run off the boat, he seems now tranquil with his new-world fate, soberly communicating to his father Fortunata's desire.

Pietro's newly found capability of speech is now juxtaposed to Fortunata's selective mutism, and both characters now switch places; Fortunata, a sort of chatterbox, as Salvatore himself said, in the old world, is silenced in/by this new world, whereas Pietro, comfortably silent as a *selective mute* in the old world, is now a speaker in this new world. Selective mutism is a disorder in both children and adults who, despite their silence, are fully capable of speech and understanding language. This, in fact, seems to be the case early on with Pietro; while he does not speak, he clearly hears and understands what people around him are saying.[26]

Pietro's country existence of desired mutism is now cancelled out; and in order for him to thrive in this new world, he must now adapt to it, and his first requirement is the adoption of language. Pietro must now rely also on language, the almighty logos, for which, as we already stated earlier, Descarthes's "Cogito ergo sum" is once again transformed into the Italian immigrant's "Parlo, dunque sono." This is also ironically underscored by Pietro's use of the word "disse." It is ironic, literally speaking, precisely because, as far as we can tell, the mode of communication at this time between Fortunata and Pietro is not linguistic, they do not actually *speak* to each other; they communicate through facial expressions and gestures. Yet, Pietro says, "la nonna mi disse." Furthermore, the very act of Pietro *saying* "la nonna mi disse" now accentuates the fact that until this point in the film Pietro had not verbally articulated any information of any sort. Thus, as viewers, we witness an ironi-

---

[26] Selective mutism is a most complex condition and puzzling to a significant degree. For more on this condition, see Spasaro and Schaefer (1999); Hadley (1994); Kratochwill (1981).

cally chiasmatic-like shifting of verbal language and gesticulating idiom, here in the visual medium of cinema, as charted below:

	Italy	United States
Fortunata	Speech — > Gestures	
	X	
Pietro	Gestures — > Speech	

As already stated above, through the character of Fortunata, we see that staunch, old-world modes of living are not suitable for the new world. Not only is this implied by the Ellis Island examiners who deem her "feeble minded" and therefore want to send her back, it is also something that Fortunata herself understands, as she now has decided to return to Italy where she will "morire a casa." Pietro, too, undergoes a similar transformation. Again, as stated earlier, his initial fear of the trip and all of its consequences are now dissipated, aware at this juncture that the new world is where he belongs — an awareness, I would underscore at this juncture, that has its origins in the old world, namely in Fortunata, as Pietro so aptly articulates: for not only does "la nonna disse che vuole morire a casa," but, more poignantly, it is indeed "la nonna" who "disse ... che noialtri dobbiamo stare accà." Ironic once more, then, is not that the new world has overwhelmed the old world; rather, the old world has succeeded in understanding the significance of the new world and the inevitable necessity to adapt to it if one so desires to dwell therein, in order for one to enjoy both a personal and economic amelioration.

THE END OF THE BEGINNING: ALL IS POSSIBLE

As I mentioned earlier in this chapter, *Nuovomondo* concentrates on the journey to and not the emigrant's life within the United States. It is, to be sure, the process that holds center stage in this film. The Mancusos and Lucy undergo a transformation during this migratory experience, one that clearly impacts their future precisely because it impacts their present-day voyage from Italy to the United States. They pass through the trials and tribulation of the risky trip over, where any and all manifestations of storms, infectious disease, and violence due to overcrowding could erupt at any minute. They also survived the "modern" vision of the bureaucracy of Ellis Island, with its doctors, professionally steeped in the theory of eugenics, who decided the fate of those who risked weeks of travel in steerage; those who believe to be "Gods who decide who is and is not fit to enter," as Fortunata underscores at the end, refusing to follow the "rules of the new world," as the Ellis Island official put it.

The final realistic scene of the film, this family portrait of the Mancusos who left Italy, dissolves into one of a river of milk, for which a number of issues come to the fore. First, the initial screen is a white blank, a sort of *tabula rasa* on which, metaphorically, our immigrants can write their new story in this new world.[27] Second, from screen right, Lucy appears and gradually moves into center screen. As she settles into this new position, three heads eventually appear from beneath the surface; Salvatore, Angelo, and Pietro. As they situate themselves, they take up the same positioning as the final portrait of the three men and their mother/grandmother. We now have in front of us a family portrait of the *new* Mancuso family, that which will inhabit the new world. In Fortunata's stead (i.e., old-world sign) we find Lucy (i.e., new-world sign), that triangular sign as mentioned earlier, whose signifying functionality is one of gender, class, and journey. She is, as we saw above, the requisite lynchpin that buttresses the various facets of the migratory experience at the opening of the twentieth century.

For more than thirty seconds the *new* Mancuso family occupies the entire screen, holding their respective positions of the original old-world family portrait, as, instead, turn of the twenty-first music plays. Once this familial image is securely imprinted into the viewer's mind, the scene begins to open up, and we now see other immigrants in the river of milk, indeed a sea of milk, eventually transforming itself into a birds-eye view of the heads/hats of these newly minted Americans, we can assume. Such a camera an-

---

[27] I remind the reader of the previous *tabula rasa*, similar for sure to this one, when the Mancusos first arrived in the city from which they eventually departed.

gle serves as a wonderful counterpoint to one of two previous birds-eye view. When the ship left the port, we saw a multitude of emigrant travelers, obviously anxious swiftly look up toward the camera as the ship's horn loudly sounded its departure. Here, it is no longer necessary for us to see their faces, since, after this earthly re-birth of theirs, in this river of milk they receive the requisite nourishment, to be followed by milk and honey, as the belief underscores, for their spiritual re-birth.[28] Furthermore, and equally poignant here in this migratory context, the apocryphal river of milk was also that place where people were eventually rewarded, as we read below:[29]

> 23. And the angel answered and said unto me: Follow me and I will bring thee into the city of Christ. And he stood by (upon) the lake Acherusa, and set me in a golden ship, and angels as it were three thousand sang an hymn before me until I came even unto the city of Christ. [...] There was a river of honey, and a river of milk, and a river of wine, and a river of oil. And I said unto the angel: What are these rivers that compass this city about? And he saith to me: These are the four rivers which flow abundantly for them that are in this land of promise, whereof the names are these: the river of honey is called Phison, and the river of milk Euphrates, and the river of oil Geon, and the river of wine Tigris. Whereas therefore when the righteous were in the world they used not their power over these things, but hungered and afflicted themselves for the Lord God's sake, therefore when they enter into this city, the Lord will give them these things without number ... and without all measure. [...]
>
> 26. Again he led me where was the river of milk, and I saw in that place all the children whom the king Herod slew for the name of Christ, and they greeted me, and the angel said unto me: All they that keep chastity in cleanness, when they are gone out of the body, after they worship the Lord God, are delivered

---

[28] See Hilda M. Ransome (1937, 280). For more, see her chapter 21, "Ritual Uses of Milk and Honey" (276-84).
[29] See the "Apocalypse of Paul" (1924, §§ 23-31).

unto Michael and brought unto the children: and they greet them saying: They are our brothers and friends and members: among them shall they inherit the promises of God.

Those rewarded in the river of milk were also children, those slain by King Herod—an appropriate metaphor, indeed, for the immigrants who, like the children, were innocent victims to circumstances beyond their control, those circumstances being both the natural disasters and socio-political players of both the old world as well as the risky voyage and eugenically based philosophy of the new world. Further still, whereas "angels as it were three thousand sang an hymn before me until I came even unto the city of Christ," here too the film closes with seven minutes of Nina Simone's classic ten-minute version of "Sinnerman," a turn-of-the-century, traditional spiritual often sung at religious rivals.

In the end, the Mancusos and all their Italian brothers and sisters who made the trip together, find themselves, at this juncture, in the "river of milk [...], delivered" into this new world where, as the viewer may now semiotically narrate, "among them shall they inherit the promises of" the new world, that "terra nuova" to which Rosa had so presciently referred earlier in the film.

WORKS CITED

"Apocalypse of Paul" in *The Apocryphal New Testament*. 1924. M.R. James, Translation and Notes. Oxford: Clarendon Press. ¶¶ 23-31.

Barolini, Helen. 1979. *Umbertina*. New York: Seaview.

Calvino, Italo. 1963. *Marcovaldo, ovvero le stagioni in città*, with illustrations by Sergio Tofano (Turin: Einaudi. In English, *Marcovaldo: Or the Seasons in the City*, tr. William Weaver. New York: Harcourt Brace Jovanovich, 1983.

Carbonara, Lorena. 2017. "Language, Silence and Translation in Emanuele Crialese's Polyglot Migration Film *Nuovomondo – Golden Door* (2006)." *Cad. Trad., Florianópolis* 37.1 (Jan.-Apr.): 119-138.

Doll, Edgar. 1917. A. *Clinical Studies in Feeble-mindedness*. Boston: Richard G. Badger.

Eco, Umberto. 1988. "*Intentio Lectoris*: The State of the Art," *Differentia, review of italian thought*. 2: 147-68.

Eco, Umberto. 1976. A Theory of Semiotics. Bloomington, IN: Indiana University Press.

Fiore, Teresa. 2017. "Realist and Magical Realist Emigration Voyages in Criaslese's *Nuovomondo*" in *Pre-Occupied Spaces: Remapping Italy's Transnational Migrations and Colonial Legacies*. The Bronx, NY: Fordham University Press. 40-49.

Geertz, Clifford. 1979. "From the Native's Point of View: On the Nature of Anthropological Understanding" in *Interpretive Social Science: A Reader*. Paul Rabinow and William M. Sullivan, eds. Berkeley: University of California Press.

Goddard, Henry Herbert. 1914. *Feeble-mindedness: Its Causes and Consequences*. New York: McMillan.

Hadley, Norman H. 1994. *A Handbook for Educators, Counselors, and Health Care Professionals*. Dordrecht & Boston: Kluwer Academic Publishers.

Heyer-Caput, Margherita. 2013. "For a Cinema of *Inbetween-ness*: Emanuele Crialese's *Nuovomondo* (2006)," *Italica* 90.2 (Summer): 272-285.

Hilda M. Ransome. 1937. *The Sacred Bee in Ancient Times and Folklore*. New York: Houghton Mifflin Co.

Kratochwill, Thomas R. 1981. *Selective Mutism: Implications for Research and Treatment*. Hillsdale, N.J.: L. Erlbaum Associates.

Lombroso, Cesare. 1902. "The Last Brigand." *La Nuova Antologia*.

Merrell, Floyd. 2003. *Sensing Corporeally: Toward a Posthuman Understanding*. University of Toronto Press. 33-51.

_____. 1991. *Signs Becoming Signs: Our Perfusive, Pervasive Universe*. Bloomington: Indiana University Press.

Michaud, Marie-Christine. 2017. "Nuovomondo, Ellis Island, and Italian Immigrants: A New Appraisal by Emanuele Crialese." *Quaderni d'italianistica* 38.1: 37–60.

Milli Konewko, Simonetta. 2015. "Emanuele Crialese's *Nuovomondo* and the Triumph of the Mediterranean Heritage." *Athens Journal of Humanities & Art* 2.4: 211-220.

Mimì metallurgico ferito nell'onore. Dir., Lina Wertmüller. 1972. Euro International Film.

Nuovomondo. 2006. Dir. Emanuele Crialese. Miramax. 1h 58 min. Released 22 September.

Peirce, Charles Sanders. 1931-1935. *The Collected Papers of Charles Sanders Peirce*. Vols. I-VI Charles Hartshorne and Paul Weiss, eds. Cambridge, MA: Harvard University Press.

Pellegrino, Francesco. 2008. "Nuovomondo: un sogno ad occhi aperti: storie di emigrazione nel film di Emanuele Crialese." *Annali della Facoltà di Scienze della formazione*. Università degli studi di Catania 7: 167-190.

Rees, A. L. and Frances Borzello, eds. 1988. *The New Art History*. Atlantic Highlands, NJ: Humanities International Press.

Spasaro, Sheila A. and Charles E. Schaefer, eds., *Refusal to Speak: Treatment of Selective Mutism in Children* (Northvale, N.J.: Jason Aronson, 1999).

Steinberg, Stephen. 1989 (1981). *The Ethnic Myth: Race, Ethnicity, and Class in America*. Boston: Beacon Press.

Tamburri, Anthony Julian. 2007a. *Narrare altrove: diverse segnalature letterarie*. Firenze: Franco Cesati Editore.

_____. 2007b. "Appunti e notarelle sulla cultura diasporica degli Italiani d'America: ovvero, suggerimenti per un discorso di studi culturali," *Campi immaginabili* 34/35: 247-64.

_____. 1994. "Centering on Nothing: Aldo Palazzeschi and Giorgio de Chirico Signing On." *Signifying Behavior. An International Journal of Semiotics* 1.1: 255-73.

Turner, Victor. 1995 (1969). *The Ritual Process: Structure and Anti-Structure*. Chicago: Aldine Transaction.

van Gennep, Arnold. 1961 (1909). *The Rites of Passage*. Chicago: University of Chicago Press.

Virga, Anita. 2018. "What Passes Through the Door: *Nuovomondo* and the Postcolonial Disruptions." *English Studies in Africa* 61.1: 55-59.

_____. 2015. "*1860* e *Nuovomondo*: due diverse 'storie' di subalterni siciliani a confronto." *Italian Studies in Southern Africa / Studi d'Italianistica nell'Africa Australe* 28.1: 62-82.

Viewing *Big Night* as Easy as One, Two, Three
A Peircean Notion of an Italian/American Identity

*You are the one! You are the one! You think things are
so simple? Huh? You think it is just like this and like
that? And there is nothing in the middle? Is that what
you think?*

—Secondo to Primo,
on the beach toward film's end

PART ONE—DEFINITIONS AND CATEGORIES

Big Night is a film about two post-war Italian immigrant brothers' struggle within the Northeastern region of the United States.
Primo and Secondo constitute a dyad that is eventually comple-
mented by yet a third person, Pascal. Together, they ultimately
complete a triad of the likes that we can find in sociological and
interpretive studies and methodologies, as shall become apparent
in the pages that follow.

Obviously, the names of the two brothers are fundamental to
any reading of this sort on both the literal and metaphorical levels:
older, younger; first course, second course; and so on.[1] They bear
witness to the types of people they each represent. In like fashion,
Pascal, too, has a name, modified as it is, that also figures ultimately
as key in my reading of this film, though not in a signifying manner
in the strictest sense of the term. Nomenclature, then, in a variety
of ways, thus proves to be fundamental in this reading, as names
are indeed other versions of signs in a basic semiotic sense.[2]

৪৹

---

[1] For those not familiar with the traditional Italian meal, it consisted of four servings: antipasto (appetizer); primo (first course, usually a pasta); secondo (a meat dish); and dessert,
fruit, and/or cheese.

[2] For an alternative reading of *Big Night*, subsequent to my initial analysis, see Lindenfeld
and Parasecoli where they consider the film, and rightfully so, as an exploration of the "the
tension between producing art and earning money in a marketplace that demands high returns" (2016, 40-41).

As I have rehearsed elsewhere, Daniel Aaron is one of the first to have dealt with the notion of hyphenation within the general discourse of American literature. For him, the hyphen initially represented older North Americans' hesitation to accept the new-comer; it was their way, in Aaron's words, to "hold him at 'hyphen's length,' so to speak, from the established community" (Aaron 1964, 213).[3] It further "signifies a tentative but unmistakable withdrawal" on the user's part, so that "mere geographical proximity" denies the newly arrived "full and unqualified national membership despite ... legal qualifications and ... official disclaimers to the contrary" (213).[4] This, of course, then sets the stage for a number of reactions on the part of the new-comer. Such social phenomena and their impact, I submit, are apparent in the storyline of the film *Big Night* (Scott and Tucci 1996). Old-world vs. new-world and Italian vs. Italian American are rolled into one, and the conflicts, negotiations, lack thereof, and potential resolutions all become apparent.

From a sociological perspective, in turn, Irvin L. Child discussed three types of individuals who inhabited at one time the Italian/American community of New Haven, Connecticut. In a study published in 1943, he spoke about three different types of reactions: "The In-group Reaction"; "The Apathetic Reaction; "The Rebel Reaction." These three categories, I would contend, have their analogies in what we shall see later in Charles Sanders Peirce's three cognitive categories.[5]

---

[3] Daniel Aaron later revised his essay (1984-85), but the substance remained the same. Hence, I quote here from the original version.

[4] Aaron is not alone in discerning this multi-stage phenomenon in the ethnic writer. Ten years after Aaron's original version, Rose Basile Green spoke to an analogous phenomenon within the history of Italian/American narrative; then, she discussed her four stages of "the need for assimilation," "revulsion," "counterrevulsion," and "rooting" (Basile Green 1974, especially chapters 4-7).

As I have already discussed in another venue (Tamburri 1991), I would contend that there are cases where a grammar rule/usage may connote an inherent prejudice, no matter how slight. Besides the hyphen, another example that comes to mind is the usage of the male pronoun for the impersonal, whereas all of its alternatives—e.g., *s/he, she/he,* or *he/she*—are shunned. See, also, Tamburri (1998, 2010).

[5] I would also point out that Child's's three stages may indeed have their analogs in the different generations that Joseph Lopreato (1970) and Paul Campisi (1948) each describe and analyze: i.e., "peasant," "first-," "second-," and "third-generation." With regard to this fourth genera-

I shall in fact start with Child's "in-group reaction," as I see it closest to Peirce's category of "firstness." The in-grouper, we are told, "strives primarily for acceptance by the Italian group and acts in such a way as to please fellow Italians rather than to gain the favor of Americans" (Child, 118). Joseph Lopreato, years later, sees this turn inward as an assertion of "the superiority [this individual sees in] his nationality group over other nationality groups" (1970, 73); and here we can readily include the so-called American nationality as well. Such a reaction, Lorpreato is convinced, "offers the individual the chance to express the hostility that accompanies his striving for group status and is heightened by frustration of that striving" (1970, 74). This, thus, brings to mind Primo, who, as shall become apparent, is obstinately tied to his Italian identity.

Child's second category that proves pertinent to this viewing/reading is his "apathetic reaction." Here, we find that the individual "retreat[s] from the conflict situation"; and in the "course of this retreat the emotional and significance of the facts and symbols of nationality building are blurred and diminished" (Child, 151). The apathy here lies in his desire not to take sides. Instead, he "feel[s] the same toward everybody" (Child, 164) and thus does not express any preference over either group. "His strategy," Lopreato believes, "is to quietly gain a certain degree of acceptance in both cultures by refusing to maintain any consistent nationality level" (Lopreato 1970, 70). Here, I have in mind Secondo, who as we shall see, is constantly trying to negotiate both the Italian and the American.

Finally, Child's third category, "the rebel reaction," is characterized by a "predominance in the individual of the tendency to achieve complete acceptance by the American group" (Child, 76). And, Child continues, "[a]ttainment of this goal requires that the individual rid himself of habits and associations that mark him as Italian and become as completely as possible an American" (Child, 76). What is also curious about this individual, according to Child,

---

tion—Lopreato's and Campisi's "third generation"—I would state here, briefly, that I see the writer of this generation subsequent to Aaron's "third-stage writer," who eventually returns to his/her ethnicity through the process of re(dis)covery.

is his conviction that his Italian-ness is "a barrier to his acceptance in American groups," and that his "effort to overcome the barrier [is] by showing that he is capable of acting like an American" (Child, 78). He is, as Lopreato also underscores, "impatient to become thoroughly American *in the shortest period possible*" (Lopreato 1970, 69-70); and he "exerts even more effort to reach the goal of higher education status" (Child, 82). Here, of course, I have in mind Pascal.

℘

What then can we finally make of these characters who seem to represent three different individuals from one person to the next? In line with Child to a certain degree, we would not err to look at these three stages from another perspective, a cognitive Peircean perspective of firstness, secondness, and thirdness as rehearsed in his *Principles of Philosophy*. All three stages, for Peirce, represent different modes of being dependent on different levels of con-sciousness. They progress, that is, from a state of non-rationality ("feeling")[7] to practicality ("experience")[8] and on to pure rationality ("thought")[9] — or, "potentiality," "actuality," and "futuribility."

If firstness is the isolated, *sui generis* mode of possibly being Peirce tells us it is, we may see an analog in Child's "in-group reaction." For it is here, Child tells us, that the individual "strives primarily for acceptance by the Italian group."[10] In this sense, his sensorial experiences, his/her "feelings," as Peirce calls them, constitute, to borrow from what Aaron stated about the first-stage writer, the "very stuff of

---

[7] "By a feeling, I mean an instance of that kind of consciousness which involves no analysis, comparison or any process whatsoever, nor consists in whole or in part of any act by which one stretch of consciousness is distinguished from another" (1.306).

[8] Secondness, as "the mode of being of one thing which consists in how a second object is" (1.24), provokes a "forcible modification of our ways of thinking [which is] the influence of the world of fact or *experience*" (1.321; emphasis textual).

[9] "The third category of elements of phenomena consists of what we call laws when we contemplate them from the outside only, but which when we see both sides of the shield we call thoughts" (1.420).

[10] I make this distinction in order not to contradict myself vis-à-vis Peirce's use of the term "real" when he discusses secondness. There, he states: "[T]he real is that which insists upon forcing its way to recognition as *something* other than the mind's creation" (1.325).

[his/her ethnic] material" (1964, 215); for he is adamant "to please fellow Italians [and remain with them] rather than to gain the favor of Americans," as we saw above with regard to Child's study. Namely, those recordings of what s/he simply experiences, without the benefit, or dare we say desire, of any "analysis, comparison or any [other] process whatsoever ... by which one stretch of consciousness is distinguished from another." While there is some sense of comparison in Child's "in-group reaction," I would beg my reader's indulgence insofar as the member of the "in group" remains indeed firmly ensconced within the group of origin, as Child tells us. That said, this person does not give in to any form of "influence" vis-à-vis his or her way of thinking that would then modify any perceptual behavioral patterns due to his "world of fact or experience," as Peirce would say.

As Child's second individual shifts from the initial stage — "that kind of consciousness which involves no analysis," or if it does, provokes no modification of behavior, Peirce would tell us — to the "apathetic," s/he now engages in some form of analysis and comparison, two processes fundamental to Peirce's secondness. This individual, that is, becomes aware of the dominant culture — "how a second object is" — and does not retreat into his original culture as does the "in-grouper." The "apathetic" individual undergoes, as Peirce would tell is, a "forcible modification of ... thinking [which is] the influence of the world of fact or *experience*." The result, then, is, as we saw above, a "retreat from the conflict situation" that subsequently blurs and diminishes the "symbols of nationality building," with the hopes, as we saw Lopreato underscore years later, of gaining "acceptance in both cultures by refusing to maintain any consistent nationality level."

Child's third category — "the rebel reaction" — transcends the first two categories of loyalty to national origin and a desire to avoid conflict precisely because he sees his national identity, as we saw above, as "a barrier to his acceptance in American groups." He is aware of the various stumbling blocks that identification with his *italianità* could create and thus is adamant at demonstrating that his is, as Child stated, "capable of acting like an American." For that "element of cognition [thirdness, according to Peirce] which is neither feeling [firstness] nor the polar sense [secondness], is the consciousness of a process, and this in the form of the sense of learning, of acquiring mental growth is eminently characteristic of cognition" (1.381). Peirce goes on to tell us that this third mode of being is timely, not immediate; it is the consciousness of a process, the "consciousness of synthesis" (1.381), which is precisely what this third-stage, individual does. S/he can transcend the intellectual experiences of the first two stages because of all that has preceded him/her.

What we now witness with these three types of Italian Americans is a progression from a stage of visceral allegiance to National identity to that of incredulous "impatien[ce] to become thoroughly American *in the shortest period possible*" (Lopreato 1970, 69-70), with passage through that secondary stage of the "apathetic" in which the individual hopes to be able to straddle the bridge between the two different cultures. In the end, then, we have three distinct phenomena of identity: (1) a strong allegiance to one's national origins; (2) in contrast, a desire to amalgamate — indeed, reconcile the differences between them — one's culture of origin with the host culture; and (3) further still, an unmitigated adherence to the host culture. Thus, we have Primo, Secondo, and Pascal, as they represent each of these three phenomena.[11]

PART TWO — VIEWING *BIG NIGHT*

Primo's ties to his national origin are manifested in numerous ways; he is indeed adamant that his situation not be changed. As a cook, for instance, he is dedicated entirely to Italian cuisine, nothing less will suffice, and no modification — read, Americanization — for any reason is acceptable to his liking; he would prefer going bankrupt than giving in to the adulteration — "rape" is his word — of what he considers to be pure Italian cuisine. A poignant scene in this regard is the customer who wished to have a side order of spaghetti with her "risotto con scampi," she being incapable of under-

---

[11] I would be remiss not to propose the notion that these three phenomena may also be present, at different stages of course, within the overall trajectory of a single writer's career. While they may indeed distinguish three different classifications of writers, they may also, conversely, characterize different stages in the development of a writer throughout his/her career.

standing that two starches, according to Italian cooking, cannot stand together.

This scene is important both on the local level vis-à vis Primo as it is on a more universal level, the comparison between Italian and American perceptions of Italian cuisine. As such, then, these differences also underscore the difference between Italian culture and American culture. In addition, they also underscore the difference between "old world" and "new world." We may indeed expand the comparison once more; for it is also a post-World War II dichotomy, one that is less related to the escape from "miseria" than it is to a desire for amelioration.[12] Nonetheless, it remains a contrast of two worlds that needs to be constantly negotiated, as would the Secondos of the world, or indeed combatted, as would instead the Primos. Further still, be it a comparison of the two worlds either during the great wave of immigration (1880-1920) or in the post-War area, the dichotomy of old-world thinking vs. new-world adventurism still exists.

The meticulousness with which Primo liberates his *risotto* in the kitchen, sprinkling on it the requisite *prezzemolo*, is counterbalanced by the female customer's initial remark about her partner's dish, which, as she says, "comes with leaves." Then, of course, there is her total ignorance of how *risotto*, a starch, as Secondo tells her, "really doesn't quite go with pasta," it, too, a starch. At this point, the man of the couple tells his female companion to order a side order of spaghetti and meatballs and that he will eat her meatballs. Here, again, there is a difference in the conceptualization of Italian food. First, we saw that Secondo used the term "pasta" whereas our American couple used the word "spaghetti." Now, given the time frame of this story's setting, in the second half of the mid-1950s, people generally spoke in terms of "spaghetti" or "macaroni." Pasta, on the other hand, was a term that was generally used within the Italian family and most likely only when speaking Italian. Secondo is Italian and thus uses the quotidian term, "pasta," that would be used in his home country of Italy.

---

[12] Regarding "miseria" and the Italian immigrant, see Lopreato (1967, *passim*).

The second difference to underscore in this scene is that spaghetti is part and parcel of that dish we know that goes by the moniker "spaghetti and meatballs." When Secondo tells his American customers that spaghetti does not come with meatballs, the female customer is incredulous because, after all, for an American mindset, the consummate Italian "pasta" (read, "spaghetti") dish is indeed "spaghetti and meatballs," that conjunction "and" being a type of conceptual super-glue for which these two elements are forever bound together, in spite of the fact that, as Secondo tells us, "sometimes spaghetti likes to be alone."

Primo's absolute loyalty to his culture's cuisine is firm during the discussion that immediately follows between him and Secondo in the kitchen. We see, first, a silent close-up of Primo with an expression of convicted resolve; he is adamant not to serve the requested side order of "spaghetti and meatballs." Primo sees such a culinary violation as a "crime" — "she's a criminal…" — against his national, and in his restaurant, unadulterated cuisine. Such a "crime" is so severe for Primo that he decides it is not worth his while to talk to her:

> No. She is a Philistine. I'm no gonna talk to her. She no understand anyway.[13]

How does this underscore relevancy of Primo's loyalty to his culture, through cuisine, to Peirce's notion of Firstness, we may continue to ask? Well, of the various definitions and explanations Peirce attributes to firstness, he also states: "The idea of First is predominant in the ideas of freshness, life, freedom. The free is that which has not another behind it, determining its actions; but so far as the idea of the negation of another enters, the idea of another enters; and such negative idea must be put in the background, or else we cannot say that the Firstness is predominant" (302). Primo indeed puts "in the background" all that which might in some way or another influence him

---

[13] As we shall see, about eight minutes after this episode (15:48) the notion of modifying Italian food as a crime arises once more.

so that the "negation of another [does not] enter": and thus, his concept of Italian cuisine maintains its characteristics of "ideas of freshness, life, freedom."

But it is not just Primo's behavior in the kitchen that is not modifiable. He tends to socialize only with Italians, hence his friendship with Alberto, their barber friend, implies either a lack of desire or an inability to discourse with Americans. One instance in which he surely desires to engage in dialogue, but finds it most difficult, is his interaction with Anne, the flower lady. Primo is so inhibited by his shyness—due in part, for sure, to his obstinacy to speak only Italian—and, as Anna Camaiti Hostert underscores, his lack of courage, that he cannot even articulate an invitation to Anne so she might attend the (in)famous dinner for Louis Prima. It is, instead, she who "is able to overcome linguistic and cultural barriers and comprehend the tenderness and the talent of this timid and awkward man."[14] But let us not lose the potentially significant valence of both Primo's shyness and consequential lack of courage as well as Anne's ability to bridge linguistic and cultural lacunae, as Camaiti Hostert states. Primo's shyness or inability to overcome his cultural fear—whichever if may be—prevents him from crossing the gendered cultural border of male-female relationships, and, as a result, he remains within his closed world of all that smacks of Italian. It is, instead, Anne who bridges the gap once she come to know that Pino would want her to come to the dinner. The overriding consequence is that Anne, an American woman, decides to cross over these socio-cultural borders in order to enter Pino's world, his culturally Italian and, we must underscore, gendered space in which he remains steadfastly ensconced.

Finally, Primo's desire to *remain* Italian, in being *and* in work, is manifested by the phone call he makes to his uncle back in Italy, expressing his desire to return to Italy and work in his uncle's new restaurant in Rome. This phone call is telling for a number of reasons; it underscores his thought process of being fixed in a pure Italian mode of cooking or nothing else at all. It also speaks to the above-implied

---

[14] See Anna Camaiti Hostert (2002).

reluctance on his part to de-Italianize himself through a modification of his thought process; his potential analysis, that is, to see the "second object [as it] is," as Peirce tells us of secondness. All of this is later underscored by the fact that Primo refuses to work for Pascal, as Pascal will later remind Secondo that he wants the two to work for him.

In the end, Primo remains fixed within the confines of his *italianità*, firm in his resolve not to be shaken from this Italian base that gives essence to his being. While he may be aware of that "other object," as Peirce states, Primo is not capable of any form of analysis that would, in the end, make him realize "how [that] second object is." As such, Primo remains well within his initial state of *italianità* that, in the end, allows no room for comparison, an analogue, to be sure, of his state of "firstness." In the end, he underscores that *prim[e]acy* of all things Italian.

℘

While Primo is securely ensconced in his Italian-ness, Secondo wants to move beyond his heritage culture; he possesses a sense of new-world adventurism that is not steeped in any notion of old-world primacy. In so doing, he takes on the role of Child's "apathetic" individual: that person for whom the "emotional and significance of the facts and symbols of nationality building are blurred and diminished" (151), as Child stated. It is not a desire to cancel out his *italianità*; rather, he wishes to avoid any semblance of conflict, treat everyone the same, and, in the end, show some form of allegiance to both his native Italian heritage and his newly found American culture.

The first example of Secondo's attempt to reconcile the two cultures is present in the above-mentioned scene of the side order of "spaghetti and meatballs." Contrary to Primo, Secondo is adamant that the customer should receive what she desires, regardless of the fact that pasta "sometimes wants to be alone." For him, the customer is always right, even if it means adulterating Italian cuisine, or, perhaps even more egregious, such as taking an item off the menu, as he suggests soon thereafter: "What do you think if we take risotto off the menu?"

> Look. *Risotto* costs us a lot. And it take you a long time to make...
> I mean, you must work so hard to make, so, then we have to
> charge more, and... these customers don't understand really what
> is a *risotto*. And so ... there always is a problem.

Secondo's suggestion is purely economical, as the ingredients are
expensive, it takes much longer to prepare than most other dishes,
and the price must be increased. In the end, Secondo underscores,
the customers are unaware of how truly different of a dish "risotto"
is. This was patently clear in the previously discussed episode, as
they did not realize that two starches do not go together. Indeed,
not only were they unaccustomed to "risotto," but the woman's
comment about her husband's pasta coming "with leaves" demonstrated how unfamiliar they were with the simple garnish of the
dish, let alone something, for the time, as different, if not as exotic,
as "risotto."

But the practicality of Secondo's suggestion is lost on Primo. In
an obvious act of ultimate and disdainful sarcasm, he suggests ever
so nonchalantly that perhaps they should substitute it with the "hot
dog," an item so much the opposite of something as ultra-Italian as
"risotto" that Primo cannot even remember — or indeed feigns not to
remember — its name in English. The two items — "risotto" vs. "hot-
dog" — represent here the polar opposites of the Italian and the
American cuisines. Primo's "in-grouper" status, in turn, is underscored by his total loyalty to his genuine Italian cuisine, as he states:
"If you give people time, they learn." And Secondo, in his very non
"in-grouper" mode of thinking responds accordingly: "I don't have
time for them to learn. This is a restaurant, not a fucking school!"
Here, let us recall, Secondo is reacting not only to Primo's response,
but, more important, to the ultimatum he was given by the bank
manager, to settle up back debts by the end of the month. It is a question of survival; and if they are to survive, they must surely, so Secondo believes, rid themselves of their "in-grouper" mode of thinking and thus adapt to a more reconciled if not totally integrated mode
of thought and action.

Yet, there is another curious aspect to the entire "risotto" episode. In traditional Italian (read, Italian/American) restaurants during what we may call the pre-*Made-in-Italy* era — whereas we can mark the beginning of the *Made-in-Italy* era with the late 1970s and early 1980s — "risotto" was not a common item on the menu.[15] Thus, the fact that it is on the restaurant's regular menu only underscores the so-called genuine Italian establishment that the brothers' restaurant Paradiso is.[16] But it is an establishment, as we shall see later on, that lacks the flare and flamboyance of Pascal's restaurant, named, of course, after its owner. With the suggestion that it be taken off the menu, Secondo engages in the typical act of the apathetic individual for whom the "the facts and symbols of nationality building are [not only] blurred [but indeed] diminished," as the suggested removal of "risotto" from the restaurant's daily menu would indeed diminish the genuine Italian aspect of Paradiso's cuisine.

Secondo's relationships with his two women may be seen, among other things, as an example of his apathetic mind-set, his in-between status that is here concretized by their presence. One is Irish/American, Phyllis; the other is Italian born, Gabriella; and they could not be more different. Phyllis is Secondo's girlfriend, the one he would eventually marry if all were to go according to plan. He clearly holds her to a certain level, as he may very well make-out with her, but he will not go beyond kissing and petting. We see this when we find them in the car. Secondo cannot have sex with Phyllis before they marry because he has not yet acquired what he obviously believes to be the requisite economic security that should accompany marriage. Yet, we should not preclude the element of the virtuous wife here, that sex with his "fiancé" is taboo, whereas sex with his "mistress" is not. Indeed, Camaiti Hostert has already underscored the requisite virginity of celluloid Italian America's wife-to-be, bringing it back, and rightfully so, to Martin Scorsese's *Who's That Knocking at My Door?* (1968),[17] where such a concept is

---

[15] Indeed, even today one may not easily find "risotto" on the regular menu of many "Italian" restaurants.

[16] I shall return later on to the name of Primo and Secondo's restaurant.

[17] See, again, Camaiti Hostert: "Once again, the stereotype of an Italian or an Italian American

brought home brutally to the "Girl" after she recounts to JR about her having been raped. For him, the fault lies with her; JR first calls her a "whore" and then decides to "forgive" her. So, with this brief reference as a backdrop, we might also assume that, while financial security may be Secondo's articulated excuse, some residue from his Italian Catholicism may also be at play here.

Gabriella, instead, is a different case for Secondo. Married, cheating on her husband, and with a healthy dose of skeptical sarcasm, she puts Secondo at ease. Here, there is no question of purity, virginity, and the like; she is married, they are involved in a secret affair. He is her opportunity to escape what we might assume is not a good marriage; she, on the other hand, for him is his outlet for his sexual desire. But the *quid pro quo* is more for him. She is, further still, useful to him in another way, as when he needs her to call the liquor salesman in order to assure delivery of inexpensive libations for the "big night." In addition, we should not ignore the fact that they are both Italians living in America, migrants, to be sure, who need to negotiate their migrant status within an American context. In this sense, we may indeed better understand their special relationship that seems to supersede the sexual and, in fact, at times seems more of a friendship than an amorous affair.[18] Her relationship with Pascal, in the end, is that one component that (a) serves as a bridge to and (b) might allow Secondo to integrate himself better into American society. Secondo does, after all, seek Pascal's consul if not assistance.

Finally, in Secondo's interest in things American, the one object that seems secondary at first glance is the Cadillac he notices while waiting for the liquor salesman to return. Bob the car salesman, in the meantime, has him sit in "next year's" car, a 1957 Cadillac coupe.

---

man whose wife-to-be has to be a virgin, following Catholic principles, as we see in Scorsese's *Who's That Knocking at my Door?*, is completely absent" (253).

[18] There is, however, the one moment in which Gabriella seems to express some feeling of resentment and/or regret for this arrangement, when Secondo is ready to leave her place just after she made the phone call to the liquor salesman. One might also recall a second ambiguous moment when Gabriella finds him in the restaurant's bathroom, after he came to know that Louis Prima was not coming to the restaurant, that it was all a ruse on Pascal's part. There they kiss, and it is surely a most tender act, one of compassion and deep feeling, not one of a sexual nature per sé.

This brief scene proves telling to be sure. First, we learn that for Secondo Italy is hopeless, there are no opportunities in Italy, there is, as he tells Bob, "nothing but history" in Italy. Second, this very car that Secondo is test driving, a black coupe, is the same model of the luxury car that appears earlier and that passed in front of Secondo as he was looking at Pascal's restaurant from afar. Thus, the American sign par excellence, the Cadillac, is further invested with yet another signifying function, that of being next year's model — a patently clear reference to the future. As a consequence, then, this sign of next year's model of a luxury American automobile is here juxtaposed to the Italian sign that is Italy, conversely invested with, as Secondo states, "nothing but history." It is yet another articulation of the old world — Italy — juxtaposed to the new world — next year's luxury American car.

§

Pascal, in turn, is the total "rebel" Italian who has become American in every way possible; he underscores Child's notion of "complete acceptance by the American group" and the need for "the individual [to] rid himself of habits and associations that mark him as Italian and become as completely as possible an American" (76). One of the first things Pascal obviously does is "rid himself of" his Italian name; he is in fact Pascal, not Pasquale. He has become a 'trace' of who he was. As he has modified the "qua" to "ca" and dropped the final vowel of his name, he has clearly eliminated that sign par excellence and thus coincidental barrier of Italian-ness that the name Pasquale represents. Further still, in choosing "Pascal," a clearly French sounding name, as opposed to a more American moniker such as Pat, a name often adopted for the Italian name, he has also placed himself at what he might have obviously considered a more prestigious level as a restaurateur especially given the time frame in which the film is set, an era in the United States when Italian cuisine did not occupy a position of prestige as did, instead, French cuisine.

Pascal's Americanization is patently clear once we are introduced to his restaurant. First, the introduction of Pascal's establishment comes immediately after the unpleasant conversation between

Primo and Secondo, which closes with Secondo's comment, "This is a restaurant, not a fucking school!" After a short pan of the outer front of the restaurant with a few couples of the close-up of a new luxury automobile, we see a close-up of Gabriella and then a very significant panning of an ultra-American couple. Second, while we do not hear anything this couple says, they represent a clear counterpoint to the previous couple we saw in Paradiso, especially the wife: she was uninformed, gauche in her smoking a cigarette while eating, and rather inarticulate in her speech pattern. Here, instead, in front of "Pascal's Italian Grotto," the camera focuses in on this most elegant couple: she in an obviously expensive dress, he in a tuxedo; both fair skinned, she the iconic blonde American of the time, clearly reminiscent of the popular American female of that period in the figures of both Marilyn Monroe and Jane Mansfield; he, tall and handsome. This scene is then capped off with a shot of the afore-mentioned brand new Cadillac driving away and a pan to a close-up of Secondo watching from afar.

As the camera then switches to Secondo, Primo joins him on the sidewalk, and we realize that they have just closed their restaurant at a time when Pascal's is just starting to buzz. The very brief conversation between the two brothers firmly underscores their internal differences that, we find out very soon, are emblematic of why "Pascal's Italian Grotto" is such a success and their Paradiso is not.

SECONDO: He's busy again tonight.
PRIMO: The man should be in prison for the food he serve.
SECONDO: People love it.

Primo's comment that Pascal "should be in prison for the food he serve[s]" only underscores Primo's adamancy not to give the customer what s/he wants but rather what he believes s/he should have *qua* Italian cuisine. As the female client in his restaurant was a "criminal," so now Pascal should be in prison for serving what he does in his restaurant.

When later that evening Secondo visits Pascal after dropping Phyllis off at home, we witness the internal setting of Pascal's restaurant and the various aspects that signal the difference between the two establishments. The first thing we see is the bright lights of and large entrance area to Pascal's Italian Grotto. This is juxtaposed to a close-up of Secondo walking toward Pascal' restaurant; the key object here is actually the backdrop that Secondo leaves behind. It is a dark street with dark storefronts one of which is Paradiso, slightly distinguishable in the background. He literally walks from out of the dark into the lights as he gets closer to Pascal's.

As Secondo then enters the restaurant, he is actually entering the world of Americanized Italian cuisine. At this juncture, what we see of this world here includes a female singer, a number of waiters carrying food, and numerous tables where people are eating. In all of this movement and sound one thing initially stands out: the food they are eating. Aside from the first table that has a large antipasto plate on it, the other food we see, both in the dishes of the second table and on the trays of the two waiters consists of abundantly filled plates of spaghetti and meatballs: that heretical dish that Primo refuses to serve in his restaurant; that act of criminality, we might underscore here, that (a) is forbidden in Paradiso and yet (b) omnipresent in Pascal's Italian Grotto. In this one culinary sign Italian food is totally Americanized. So, in turn, is Italian culture Americanized with the singer's presence. Performing a classic Italian song, she does so (a) with an American accent, and (b) to an Americanized rhythm that is, in addition to being out of tune, no longer the traditional slower cadence that one would readily expect.

Finally, there is the lighting. While Paradiso has regular lighting, where all is easily visible, and the tables are covered with white tablecloths, Pascal's Italian Grotto is shrouded in red: the tablecloths are red, the lighting is red, and the waiters wear red jackets.[19] The distinction is uncanny, as the seemingly potential paradisiacal white

---

[19] We are immediately reminded of Scorsese's *Mean Streets* (1973). Red has its own significance in this and a few other films of his. In discussing Scorsese's use of colors, Roger Ebert states: "The film uses lighting to suggest his slanted moral view. The real world is shot in ordinary colors, but then Charlie descends into the bar run by his friend Tony, and it is always bathed in *red*, the color of sex, blood and guilt" (emphasis added). See, Roger Ebert, review of *Mean Streets* (December 31, 2003), http://www.rogerebert.com/reviews/ great-movie-mean-streets-1973.

of the brothers' Paradiso is juxtaposed to Pascal's Italian Grotto's red, so that typical sign functions of the colors—white is purity; red, while possessing an array of meanings and symbolism, signals, among other things, seduction, immorality, and sin.

As such then, we might say that, according to Primo's mode of thought, Pascal's Italian Grotto is thus guilty ("he should be in prison") of seducing Americans into a deliberate violation of a culinary, moral principle that might very well be articulated as, "Do not adulterate Italian cuisine!" The high principle of Paradiso's philosophy of not adulterating Italian cuisine is thus juxtaposed to the unforgivable culinary transgression of Pascal's Italian Grotto, where the restaurants' actual names may also underscore such difference: the genuine and divine in "paradise" vs. the human and artificial in "grotto."

As we become more familiar with Pascal, we also come to realize how adamant he is to make it in America. He has Americanized his restaurant so that it may appeal to the American customer who is used to the "spaghetti and meatball" cuisine and not the "arborio" rice that "doesn't go really with pasta," as Secondo told his female customer at the beginning of the film. He is also determined to have both Primo and Secondo work for him. Indeed, be it for this goal in itself or, just as plausible, some sense of vengeance because of the relationship between Secondo and Gabriella, Pascal sets up Primo and Secondo to fail. With the pretext of inviting Louis Prima for a special evening that would then save the Paradiso, the brothers invest their last dollars in creating a most delightful and, dare we say, elegant and exquisite dinner that is truly second to none. But Louis Prima, as we know, never comes, and the brothers, as we can only assume, will most likely have to close the restaurant.

What becomes significant at this juncture is the conversation that transpires between Secondo and Pascal at the end of the film. It is here that we come to understand Pascal's notion of his total immersion into America, which ranges from his obnoxious use of the "f-word" with every sentence he seems to utter to his ruthless business dealings, all of which are done at whatever cost necessary:

SECONDO: You would never have my brother! He live in a world above you! What he has... what he is... is rare. You ... are nothing.

PASCAL: I am a businessman. I am anything I need to be, at any time. Tell me, what exactly are you?

This exchange underscores the crux of the film's implicit question of identity in *sensu amplo* and how we negotiate it. From the very beginning we were confronted with identity through food. Now, in spite of the fight he just had with his brother, and in underscoring family ties, Secondo defends Primo at all costs; Primo is "rare," he is unique, and, we might even say, inimitable. As such, however, within this world of Americanization, he remains unchangeable and thus at great risk as he sees everything in black and white. Secondo realized this early on and, during the fight scene a few minutes before his encounter with Pascal, so criticized his brother: "You think it is just like this and like that? And there is nothing in the middle? Is that what you think?"[20]

At this juncture of our analysis, there is a curious reference to the notion of "nothing" that we can briefly unpack from a Peircean perspective. Peirce saw "nothing" as the "not having been born"; and thus its "absolute undefin[ability] and unlimited possibility [constitutes its] boundless possibility," or better, "boundless freedom" (Peirce: CP 6.217). It is a "nothing" that nevertheless still signifies; it signifies *no thing*: namely, no one specific thing.[21] Thus, *nothing* is unlimited potentiality for the unlimited generation of *some thing* — i.e.,

---

[20] See Camaiti Hostert on the film's closing scene: "Primo returns to the kitchen and they eat next to each other. At that point the film ends with an obviously very Italian overture to the importance of familial bonds. Secondo puts his arm around his brother, indicating a tie that cannot be broken by differences of opinion or economic ruin" (255).

[21] Peirce goes on to say: "I say that nothing necessarily resulted from the Nothing of boundless freedom. That is, nothing according to deductive logic. But such is not the logic of freedom or possibility. The logic of freedom, or potentiality, is that it shall annul itself. For if it does not annul itself, it remains a completely idle and do-nothing potentiality; and a completely idle potentiality is annulled by its complete idleness (CP 6.219). I do not mean that potentiality immediately results in actuality. Mediately perhaps it does; but what immediately resulted was that unbounded potentiality became potentiality of this or that sort — that is, of some quality" (SP 6.220; emphasis textual).

the signified, meaning, interpretation, which is real, for the reader, only insofar as it is "semiotically real."[22] Or, to paraphrase Pascal, "any thing." In this sense, then, Pascal is Peircean; he has understood. Thus, contrary to Primo, who in his *rareness* will remain immutable and thus at great risk of survival in America, Pascal through his *nothing*ness, will become, as Child stated, "as completely as possible an American" (1943, 76) through his adaptability, and whenever such mutability is appropriate. He is a "businessman[; anything he] need[s] to be, at anytime," in both the literal and metaphorical sense.[23] Successful in his personal negotiations with the host culture, he becomes as successful in business. He becomes, that is, thoroughly American; he is the *ne plus ultra* of the process of Americanization, all that we have witnessed herein, which ultimately leads to the question of signification *qua* identity.

There is one other point to Pascal's notion of identity and its relationship to his name. As we saw above, he claims to be "anything he] need[s] to be." This chameleon-type aspect of his self-awareness is, I would contend, also a type of rebirth, a process of change according to the exigencies at hand. It is a mechanism that may indeed require an abandonment of original cultural traits and practices, as we saw above: namely, his desire "to become thoroughly American"

---

[22] With regard to the "actually real" vis-à-vis the "semiotically real," once again, I cite Floyd Merrell (1991): "This tree, what exactly do we see when we see it as tree? Our experience of it suggests at first blush purely immediate and perceptual awareness, devoid of all hypothetical elements. Attending more carefully to this percept reveals that our sensation reveals a more complex shape, colored patches, gentle to-and-fro motion, and so on. Combining these sensations into a whole by no means produces a 'tree.' We automatically, by embedded, habitual, inferential processes, endow the tree with a solid constituence beneath the bark, a root structure concealed beneath the surface of the ground, an obverse side which is not seen but is presupposed to be roughly comparable to the side of the 'tree' open to view, and so on, even though there is no immediate empirical evidence for some of these inferences. We also assume the tree has self-identity, a certain permanence of existence. We ordinarily take it for granted that when we are not looking at the tree, it is there nonetheless. In short, we automatically go 'beyond the information given.' This act or 'construction' converts a complex of sensations into a 'semiotically real' thing" (197; Merrell's emphasis). See also note 15 of the previous chapter.

[23] Again, I cite Peirce: "Of the three Universes of Experience familiar to us all, the first comprises all mere Ideas, those airy nothings to which the mind of poet, pure mathematician, or another might give local habitation and a name within that mind. Their very airy-nothingness, the fact that their Being consists in mere capability of getting thought, not in anybody's Actually thinking them, saves their Reality" (CP 6.455).

(Lopreato 1970, 69-70). It is, as we also witnessed, something that both Primo and Secondo cannot, or do not wish to, do, which distinctly sets them apart from Pascal. Thus, at this juncture, then, and continuing to speak in terms of rebirths—which, as just said, Pascal indeed represents as much in his Americanization—then we would not err to see yet another meaning to his name; and in this case his Italian name more than his Americanized one. Pasquale has at its root "pasqua" ("Easter"), a time of rebirth. That said, then, such a name here would have two references, not one: the first, a reference to his own success (read, rebirth) in diminishing all signs of his Italian-ness in order to become as American as possible; the second, his desire to "help" the two brothers and, consequently, allow them to enjoy—a process that Pascal, now the American, envisions, and not Primo and Secondo—their own "rebirth" in this their second chance in the restaurant business.

SOME NOT-SO-FINAL MUSINGS

In re-thinking the "big night," and in reconsidering not only Pascal's treacherous act of ruining the Paradiso restaurant financially, but also the significance of his choosing someone like Louis Prima as pretext, we are left to wonder what exactly might we infer, in the end, from this movie. Or, better still, we might ask, Who is Louis Prima in this film? What does he signify? Well, in one sense, he represents that bridge between the two cultures. With his music, he succeeded in being both American, with Jazz, and Italian, with his folkloric and popular Italian and Italianate songs. For him to be the fulcrum on which the brothers' ultimate success depended ties right into who they were and what they may or may not have had to have done in order to succeed.

But, as we saw, Louis Prima never comes. And in spite of the excellent dinner the brothers have prepared and served to the gastronomic delight of their guests, they end up broke, a commercial failure, so it seems in the end. This is indeed one reading of Louis Prima's absence: for he is the successful synthesis of the two cultures—e.g., his many best-selling albums, his contracts in Las Vegas, his numerous appearances on the Ed Sullivan Show, much of which is couched in the Italian hue with which he has invested much of his music—he is that synthesis of bi-cultural co-existence that the brothers here—indeed, more Primo, as he is the "in-grouper"—cannot achieve. Thus, Louis Prima's absence signals the imminent challenge and/or success of the immigrant experience. As such, then, the triad of Primo, Secondo, and Pascal may offer, at best, one blueprint for possible success.

WORKS CITED

Aaron, Daniel. 1964. "The Hyphenate Writer and American Letters," *Smith Alumnae Quarterly* (July): 213-7; later revised in *Rivista di Studi Anglo-Americani* 3.4-5 (1984-85): 11-28.

Big Night. 1996. Dirs. Stanley Tucci, Campbell Scott. Rysher Productions, Timpano Productions. 1h 49 min. Released 20 September.

Camaiti Hostert, Anna. 2002. "Big Night, Small Days" in *Screening Ethnicity: Cinematographic Representations of Italian Americans in the United States.* Anna Camaiti Hostert & Anthony Julian Tamburri, eds. West Lafayette, IN: Bordighera Press. 253-54.

Campisi, Paul. 1948. "Ethnic Family Patterns: The Italian Family in the United States," *The American Journal of Sociology* 53.6 (May).

Child, Irvin L. 1943. *Italian or American? The Second Generation in Conflict.* New Haven: Yale University Press.

Green, Rose Basile. 1974. *The Italian-American Novel: A Document of the Interaction of Two Cultures.* Madison, NJ: Fairleigh Dickinson University Press.

Lindenfeld, Laura and Fabio Parasecoli. 2016. *Feasting Our Eyes: Food Films and Cultural Identity in the United States.* New York: Columbia University Press. For *Big Night*, 33-48.

Lopreato, Joseph. 1967. *Peasants No More: Social Class and Social Change in an Underdeveloped Society.* San Francisco: Chandler Publishing Co.

_____. 1970. *Italian Americans.* New York: Random House.

Merrell, Floyd. 1991. *Signs Becoming Signs: Our Perfusive, Pervasive Universe.* Bloomington: Indiana University Press.

Peirce, Charles Sanders. 1960. *Principles of Philosophy* in *Collected Papers*, eds., Charles Hartshorne and Paul Weiss, Vol. 1. Cambridge, MA: Harvard University Press.

Tamburri, Anthony Julian. 2010. *Una semiotica dell'etnicità. Nuove segnalature per la scrittura italiano/ americana.* Franco Cesati Editore.

———. 1998. *A Semiotic of Ethnicity: In (Re)cognition of the Italian/American
Writer.* Albany, NY: SUNY Press.

———. 1991. *To Hyphenate or not to Hyphenate: the Italian/American Writer:
Or, An* Other *American?* Montreal: Guernica Editions.

Food as Delineator in *Dinner Rush*:
A Semiotic of Generational Difference
Among "Italians" in America

PREMISE

Like other films dealing with food, Bob Giraldi's *Dinner Rush* (2000) connotes and hence discusses food as both identity marker and indicator for shifts in generational dynamics among Italians in America, especially between father and son. My use of the term "Italians in America" encompasses those who were born and raised in Italy, and who then moved to the United States, and, as well, those who are descendants of Italian immigrants. *Dinner Rush* also deals with the identity of Italians in America as members of organized crime, this too a signifier for generational difference and, we might also say, food.[1] Hence, I have in mind the famous scene in *The Godfather* (1972) when Clemenza gives Michael a quick lesson in making pasta sauce, or, even later, the scene in *Goodfellas* (1989) where Paulie is preparing dinner while in jail, carefully slicing and dicing garlic with a razor blade. These are just two of a plethora of scenes in American films that include indelible Italian/American food scenes.[2]

As I move forward in my analysis of the film, I wish to underscore further my terminology here with regard to the phrase, "Italians in America." The issue here is that I am not dealing with any notion of what some might call "real" or "authentic" Italian food. Nor do I wish to distinguish between "real" and/or "authentic" Italians.[3] Indeed, such adjectives conjure up notions of superiority, if not simply exclusion, vis-à-vis that which is not then considered to be "real" or "authentic"; we have seen much too much of this throughout the twentieth- and into the twenty-first century. This

---

[1] See Calabretta-Sajder for more on organized crime in *Dinner Rush*.
[2] On Italian food in the U.S., see, among others, Cinotto (2013).
[3] On the notion of "real" Italians, see Ruberto and Sciorra (2017a, "Introduction").

dichotomy indeed continues today willy-nilly with the existence of organizations that consider themselves predominantly if not exclusively Italian. One that comes to mind is ISSNAF (Italian Scientists and Scholars in North America Foundation) whose mission is "to promote scientific, academic and technological cooperation amongst *Italian researchers and scholars active in North America and the world of research in Italy*" (emphasis added), as it states on its website. It is an organization that caters entirely, or so it seems, to Italians who are in some manner affiliated with a North American institution. Indeed, a key phrase of theirs seems to be the recurrent "in [or between] Italy and North America" or some variant thereof. The moniker "Italian American" in either adjectival or substantive form seems not to exist. Further still, ISSNAF seems to be STEM oriented and hence allowing some but notably little space for the humanities. In stating the above, my intention here is not to engage in a critique of such an organization, the grouping of nationals from one country—Italy—who are working in another—United States. However, I realize that in pointing out the exclusionary aspect of ISSNAF might readily be taken as a criticism of the organization. My point is that such entities that underscore the social and the somatic contribute perforce to such a distinction and/or separation as I point out here.

Instead, I submit that when dealing with any aspect of the Italian diaspora—indeed, members of ISSNAF qualify as members of a diaspora—we need to think in terms of difference, for sure; but any reference to terminology that is comparatively evaluative, if not exclusionary, smacks of arrogance and, consequently by its very usage, denigration of the progeny that is the emigrant. This is what one does, albeit *nolens volens,* when s/he adopts such linguistic registers. This, I would further contend, is one of the primary rhetorical and/or conceptual steps we need to take in this post-modern condition during this second decade of the third millennium if we are to free ourselves from the prison-house of restrictive and *de facto* hegemonic terminology, one of those grand narratives' conceptual totalitarianisms vis-à-vis notions of "Italian" identity. Yes, I am purposefully channeling Francois Lyotard and his postmodern notion of "incredulity toward grand narratives" (xiv) and the further "[de-]legitimation [of] grand narratives" (51).

That said, my use of the term "Italian" — adjective or noun — has as its possible referents all that which is/can be considered "Italian" in the United States or elsewhere outside of Italy for that matter. Further still, I realize that my desire not to distinguish such difference by way of quotation marks and the like may very well create some confusion within a reader/viewer's mind with regard to the polarity one readily perceives in Italian vs. Italian American. But that confusion, I underscore, is purposeful; the very confusion it may provoke could, I would hope, cause my reader/viewer to think twice about the two terms and hence ponder what s/he considers to be the difference that s/he perceives. In so doing, I would hope that the confusion *qua* bewilderment might, even in the most minimal of ways, transform itself into *con*-fusion *qua* bringing closer together what Peirce would call the interpretants of the signs /Italian/ and /Italian American/.

In *Dinner Rush*, Louis, the father of an aspiring *nouveau* Italian cuisine chef Udo, suffers the loss of his old friend and business partner to a criminal element because of gambling difference and turf. At the same time, Louis is bent on retiring and giving over his restaurant to Udo. Throughout the film, a series of seemingly unrelated episodes speaks to the notion of ethnic identity and generational differences through the sign functions we can readily assign to food.[4]

One of the outstanding motifs in *Dinner Rush* is the difference in the conceptualization of Italian food. Whereas in most films we witness the difference between "Italian" and "Italian-American" food, such as in Scott and Tucci's *Big Night*, in *Dinner Rush* the difference in types is one among "Italian-American" cuisine in the "traditional" sense, one might say "Americanized" Italian cuisine — and not just meatballs but also a plate of hot sausage and peppers — and a newly stylized "Italian" cuisine that is not much different from what

---

[4] Calabretta-Sajder speaks to three characteristics of food: (1) collateral, (2) character, and (3) aphrodisiac.

one might witness today in some of the more exclusive, trendy Italian restaurants of metropolitan areas such as New York City, especially within the borough of Manhattan. I would contend, further still, that the presence of "sausage and peppers" in *Dinner Rush* as opposed to "spaghetti and meatballs" is in line with the notion of a more stylized Italian cuisine we are to find in Udo's kitchen. For it is Udo himself who underscores the rejection of such a dish when, at the beginning of the film he states to his father in a retort, "We don't make meatballs here anymore!" Yet, it is also Udo who "allows" the sausage and peppers" to be cooked "in [his] kitchen," as we witness soon after this scene with his father.

VIEWING *DINNER RUSH* 1

Among the many significant scenes pertinent to my viewing, two stand out as a hint to things being quite different. First, at one point, a bit less than mid-film, Ken Roloff makes a most telling statement:

> I'm just curious here, watching all these people, star-gazing potential. I wonder, I wonder when it all changed…. When did eating dinner become a Broadway show?

Eating hence is no longer for mere sustenance; it is "a Broadway show," indeed, a performance, as is apparent throughout the film, executed not only by those who eat but, perhaps even more significant, by those who prepare the food. To be sure, "star-gazing potential" calls to mind the art critic and the latest artist he is promoting and takes to dinner at Gigino's. In like fashion, it also refers to Udo, the "star chief," as he is called by Nicole, for instance. It is thus a two-way street: the art critic, already a famous individual in his own right, comes to Udo's restaurant precisely because Udo, as well, is a star in his own right. The "star-gazing potential" is hence both internal and external. Finally, with regard to a performance, let us not forget Roloff's presence, his reason for being at Gigino's; he too is playing a role, he is a Wall-Streeter who is also an assassin. Indeed, it is ironic to be sure that Roloff poses the question. For it is he who actually has two roles—he engages in two distinct performances, we can readily state—among which he alternates according to the role necessary for the moment and where: "I could have done this in Queens," he says at the end of the movie to Louis. But as we know by now, Louis had his own reasons for the assassination to take place in Manhattan, in the restaurant he just signed over to Udo. Second, the difference between the stridently traditional Italian/American cuisine and the nouveau Italian cuisine is underscored during the opening scene.

The contemporary kitchen that is managed by Udo is juxtaposed to the traditional food that is Duncan's, and the distinction between the two cuisines is now immediately underscored for the spectator.[5] Because of its novelty—and, dare we add, complexity of its preparation—we might better understand the nouveau cuisine by seeing how it is made. Hence, we are witness at the opening of the film to the readying of the dishes, as those scenes alternate with the lunch conversation between Louis and his friends eating a meal prepared by Duncan. That said, then, whereas with regard to Duncan's cooking, we only need to see the finished product because, traditional that it is, we should already know how it is made, we actually need, instead, to see the nouveau cuisine being prepared. Further still, in order to bring greater attention to this new cooking process and also facilitate better our understanding, the kitchen scene is in slow motion.

Another aspect to this scene with regard to old world vs. new world is the conversation about nicknames. Such a practice is common among Italian and Italian Americans, especially those of a certain generation. Hence, used here by Louis and his friends only underscores their position in this film as part of the old world. The third aspect of this scene that subtends the entire narrative of the film is the reference to Louis and Enrico's bookmaking and their

---

[5] Also anticipated here—and we come to understand it better in retrospect—is the notion of identity and its origin; namely, it is a question of nature or nurture. With regard to literature, I first dealt with this unusual mode of interpretation in my study on retrospective reading (1990) and, subsequently, in a book on Aldo Palazzeschi, Guido Gozzano, and Italo Calvino (2003).

issues with Carmen and Paolo, a.k.a., Black and Blue. At first blush it is not clear how seriously dangerous this relationship might be. But very soon after Enrico leaves to pick up his granddaughter from school, we come to understand that it is, to be sure, lethal. The sociopath that he is, Paolo takes delight in killing Enrico, and it matters not that he shoots him in the back, a proverbially cowardly act that only sheds greater light on the inhumane character to Paolo and, by extension, his partner / brother-in-law, Carmen.

While the difference between the two cuisines is underscored at the opening of the film, our first overt clash between these divergent cuisines takes place during the conversation between father and son at the Louis's private table. The two contrasting cuisines are clearly distinguished in this scene by Louis's dramatic reading of the menu in the most sarcastic of manners. What is poignant at this juncture is Louis's animated reaction. While at the opening of the film his tone is matter of fact, here his attitude is spiritedly caustic. Further still, we come to understand, from Udo's own distinction ("Gabriel and a pair of Latinos you don't know.") that one need not be Italian in order to cook well Italian food. There is, in this regard, an irony to what follows:

> LOUIS: "Of course, why would there be Italians in an Italian kitchen? Of course, you've got the money."
> UDO: "Why do I have to come to the Godfather's table begging all the time?
> LOUIS: "It's tough being a star, isn't it?"
> [...]
> UDO: "Why don't you stick to the bookmaking and let me run this business?"

This conversation references *in nuce* the basic themes of the movie. Identity and the correlation Italian cuisine equals Italian chefs resonates in Louis's sarcastically rhetorical question of the need for "Italians in an Italian kitchen." Such sarcasm assists in setting up the irony we will soon perceive in Duncan's presence and in his semiotic function in the movie. Udo's coming then "to the Godfather's table begging" for money reminds us that there is also an organized crime element to the movie's narrative. Both the notion of nouveau cuisine and organized crime, and the inter-related nexus, are included in Udo's question, "Why don't you stick to the bookmaking and let me run this business?"; it solidifies the pairing and puts the spectator on notice that something related, and unpleasant to be sure, may come to pass. That said, I would further suggest that this scene is also a moment for other semiotic potentiality. There are two businesses associated with the restaurant: food and bookmaking. These two commercial fields are indeed represented here in their distinction: Udo in his white chef's coat, and Louis in his business suit. It is this second commercial attire, Louis's suit, that affords us the possibility to think distinctively. When Udo states that Louis should leave the running of the restaurant to him—"… let me run *this* business?" (emphasis mine)—it is his use of the demonstrative adjective "this" that further underscores the existence of two divergent business practices under the same roof and, more significantly, that the one (bookmaking) may not be consonant with the other (restaurant).

Louis goes on to tease Udo about the fancy items on his menu, to which Udo responds, "It's something for the critics, come on." It's something, Udo is telling his spectator as well, about how his cuisine—his readying of the various exotically named dishes—is, indeed, part of a performance. Why else, we must ask, would Udo do something for the critics if not then to receive from them the proverbial A+ for an excellent performance? Roloff's statement about going out to eat as a "Broadway show" clamors loudly in this exchange between Louis and Udo, even if ever so retrospectively. Louis then goes on to tell Udo that his "mother made food, not for the critics, simply elegant, this place smelled like heaven." And after a brief exchange, with Louis at a loss for words, Udo asks if he is seeking something "traditional," to which Louis animatedly responds, "Yes, traditional, substantial, something that tastes great, that smells great." Then, in immediate and total exasperation, he asks where Duncan is. How ironic, to be sure, that it is, indeed, Louis's own exasperation in seeking out Duncan at the end of this scene that cancels out his previous rhetorical and, to be sure, skeptical question of a cook's ethnic background, and thus identifies Duncan, a Latino, with, in Louis's own words, "traditional, substantial" Italian food.

VIEWING *DINNER RUSH* 2

While Duncan is preparing Louis's favorite dish, the brief exchange between Udo and Duncan underscores the difference in the two cuisines in question and Udo's seeming disregard for "tradition." But it also allows us to see Duncan in one of his changing roles as [sous] chef, in this instance preparing the traditional dish of sausage and peppers for Louis, something that Udo clearly allows in spite of his statement to the contrary. In fact, in a seemingly insignificant moment, as this scene ends, we hear though do not see Udo, saying "Don't burn the sausage!" This, in turn, is yet another telling sign that the gap the viewer might perceive at first blush between both the two cuisines, as well as between Udo and Duncan, is not as wide as it may seem between these two. We understand as much when Udo, having heard that Duncan is looking elsewhere, warns Duncan of two things: (1) his potentially new boss with not "put up with your shit like [he] does"; and (2), more significant, Udo denigrates the other restaurant's menu as "old, old-fashioned, heavy." Duncan's contribution to Udo's nouveau Italian cuisine is, for Udo, obviously important, this is patently clear at this juncture, otherwise Udo would not try to convince him not to leave. Further still, we also readily perceive that Duncan is here to stay, ready and willing to be part of the aforementioned "Broadway show." What we also see here is that not only is Duncan important for the restaurant's success, but it is indeed Duncan who takes over the conversation:

> UDO: Let me tell you something about this guy, the food is old, old fashion, heavy. It would be a stupid move on your part, don't do it.
>
> DUNCAN: Fuck Bulard, okay? We're turning covers like crazy, more people are going to get laid upstairs than in the last ten years. Udo, cógelo suavecito! [lit., "Take it easy!"] Relax!

In a moment when Udo is lecturing Duncan on why he should not quit to go elsewhere, Duncan's response is anything but the expected explanation / excuse of why he had an interview with Bulard. To be sure, he doesn't even address the issue. Instead, he takes over the conversation and, in sidelining the discussion about his job interview, he demonstrates an awareness of what is going on in the restaurant as far as covers are concerned. Duncan now tells Udo how good of an evening they are having, that the number of dinners is impressive, and he caps it all off with an exhortation to relax! This scene, I would contend, underscores the greater similarities between Duncan and Udo, something that we witness later on in the movie. This is that moment, I would suggest, where both Udo and Duncan are on the same level, one encouraging the other and, in the end, both in agreement.

The symbiotic relationship between Udo and Duncan manifests itself in their co-creation of the lobster/pasta dish for the food critic, a sort of dance in which they engage, each one indispensable to the other in order to complete the project. We witness a precision to their preparation of this special dish. Further still, it is not always clear who is mixing the cream sauce or who is heating the champagne. Such uncertainty and/or ambiguity can be perceived as a momentary melding of the two, the one complementing the other in order to form a whole. In addition, there are two seemingly insignificant moments that prove instead most relevant as underlying signage. The first image of this approximately three-minute-long scene is a camera scan after we see the spaghetti in the deep fryer. The camera scans half the kitchen to the stairwell where we see Nicole who stops at the bottom of the stairwell and observes the two in action without saying a word to either of them. And if we take close notice, we see that her eyes scan to her left, which is toward Duncan, a glance accompanied by a nondescript smile.

Just as Nicole arrives, both Duncan and Udo are, momentarily, framed by the top shelves of the steel table, a portrait for her to observe, we might assume. But they are also framed for us the viewers, so we, as well, see them now no longer as the apparent competitors they seemed to have previously been. Instead, they now constitute a symbiotic pair that works perfectly well together in their preparation of the special dish for the food critic, Jennifer Freely, and her friend the food nymph. The camera then scans back toward Udo and Duncan in a side view, the two alone on screen and in this moment metaphorically framed, after which the camera then returns to Nicole who now looks at the both of them, but this time with no smile, after which she readily heads back upstairs.

The framing of Udo and Duncan continues. Once Nicole leaves, the steel table's top shelves momentarily frames them once more. The camera then immediately switches to one of them—we do not know which—as one—the other?—of them, again unidentified, resumes the preparation over the stove. We see only parts of them—e.g., hands, arms, torso—and we see the food, and for the moment we do not know who is who and who is preparing which part of the meal. The only marker here we do have is Udo's bracelet as he breaks up the lobster and, a few moments later, sprinkles caviar over the finished dish.

There is a third quick framing of the two when Paolo exits the kitchen after having complimented Duncan on the *bistecca alla fiorentina*. This scene figures of import because it is Udo who tells Paolo he cannot be in the kitchen, almost as if to protect indirectly Duncan from his presence, a forecasting of the possible physical altercation to take place between the two.

The fourth and final framing of our two chefs occurs as they finish up the preparation of the special dish for the food critic. This framing is from the top, a bird's eye view as we now see them, momentarily, shoulder to shoulder to each other, and, then, Udo finishes the special meal and Duncan places the vegetables in the serving dish. The scene then immediately switches to a close-up of each of them, as Udo rounds the steel table to go upstairs with both dishes in hand and turns back to Duncan to thank him seriously, as Duncan, in turn, in a close up states with a seemingly mischievous smile, "I love it when you talk dirty, baby." Calabretta Sajder sees this as an example of "the sexual nature food can and indeed does produce" (205). By all means! Such interpretation is further signaled by a number of scenes, one of which is when the "food nymph" takes at least three sucks on the fettuccine to get it all into her mouth, each suck accompanied by a moan of a distinct sexual nature. In the same manner, however, I do wonder if we might not see a hint of homo-eroticism in this statement, given the complex relationship between Udo and Duncan as chefs and, to boot, the two of them as concurrent lovers of Nicole: a complementarity at this juncture of a much more complex nature. The fundamental complementarity of the two chefs is of course suggested early on in the movie, as I mentioned above, as we saw in the scene where Udo believes he must convince Duncan to stay. Such complementarity, I would contend—conscious for sure on Udo's part—is further punctuated twice in all of this: (1) when Udo throws Paolo out of the kitchen, and (2) when Udo, with both plates in hand, as just mentioned, stops and turns to thank Duncan in the most profuse of ways, by simply stating, "Duncan, thanks!"

The relationships that both Udo and Duncan have with Nicole create a complex and curious situation. Curious because it piques our interest and arouses our desire to scrutinize such a triad; complex for all the obvious reasons among which the two men are engaged in an affair with the same woman and they all work in the same restaurant. Further still, these relationships take place in an uneven work environment, as Udo is the son of the owner and, de facto, both Nicole's and Duncan's supervisor. So, at first blush, it seems to be a situation that is, to use a description by Mookie in Spike Lee's *Do the Right Thing*, nuclear.

Thinking now just in terms of logistics and physicality, all three characters involved in this double-layered affair constitute to a certain degree a trinity, with Nicole as the uniting figure. During the time span in which the movie takes place, Nicole and Udo engage in sex in the office off the kitchen at the beginning of the evening. Duncan is aware of as much when he arrives and goes in to change his clothes; he finds Nicole's earrings. In the course of the evening Duncan and Nicole will also engage in two secret meetings one of which ends in sexual intimacy. Noteworthy, as well, is that these two meetings take place outside of the restaurant; their tryst is off site. Nicole, as just mentioned, is the central figure, the lynchpin, if we may use such a term, in this complicated situation. She is, one might surmise, the literal intermediary between Udo and Duncan. As the two chefs sustain each other in their profession, they oddly gain strength as well in their individual relationship with Nicole, each wanting it to continue.[6] This, of course, can lead us to see this triangle as a metaphorical ménage à trois, which actually encourages the two men to try to keep alive each one's relationship with Nicole.[7]

The complexity then is also in the spatiality of what we can categorize as the "once removed." Namely, as Udo and Duncan each engage in their physical relationship with Nicole—and each one is aware of the other's liaison—then the desire to continue with Nicole is, once removed, a desire to be indirectly engaged, albeit metaphorically, with each other on this level as well as all the others. Still, and, again, metaphorically speaking, we are also in the realm of the androgyne, "the One which contains the Two" (Singer 6). According to Aristophanes in Plato's *Symposium*, this is the eventual re-merging of the two original halves of the androgyne, having been previously cut in two by Zeus:

> ... the purely sexual pleasures of their friendship could hardly account for the huge delight they take in one another's company. The fact is that both their souls are longing for a something ... to which they can neither of them put a name, and which they can only give an inkling of in cryptic sayings and prophetic riddles ... (Plato, 192 c-e; emphasis added)

Such re-merging demonstrates "how far back we can trace our *innate love* for one another, and how this love is always trying to

---

[6] It is true that one might see the relationship between Nicole and Duncan a stronger one. One might also assume that the relationship is more important for Duncan than for Udo, as Udo is most complacent at the end of the evening when Nicole tells him that the relationship between her and Duncan is "serious."

[7] Udo as "star chef" will eventually choose his role as celebrity over his relationship with Nicole, as we saw in the end, also because his role as a culinary creative genius also gets him special attention from women, as we know from the back story with other women as well. In this sense, Udo is a Lothario type, one of a few unpleasant characteristics he seems to possess.

redintegrate our former nature, *to make two into one*" (Plato 191d; emphasis added). This is yet another question, I contend, that is begged by Duncan's seemingly ludic response, "I love it when you talk dirty, baby." It calls to the fore the signficability of text with regard to either, if not both, the androgynous or the homoerotic. The jury, I would submit, is out on the final deliberation of the text's significability in this regard.

VIEWING *DINNER RUSH* 3

The Assassination scene at the end of the movie proves equally constitutive as fertile ground for a broad range of potential significability of this cinematic text. First, I would point to a more curious use of Italian toward the end of the film; and to a certain degree, it goes beyond code-switching and, to be sure, we might speak in terms of intentionality shifting from that of the character—this would be a narrator internal to the text, the homodiegetic, overt narrator—to that of an unidentified "narrator"—this would be a narrating voice external to the text, the heterodiegetic, covert narrator. When Black and Blue go to Louis's favorite spot to talk, which is in the basement in front of the toilet, a number of questions are begged at this juncture. First, we have the juxtaposition of the importance of a topic at hand being discussed—in this case Black and Blue wanting to take both the bookmaking business and the restaurant—in the basement and, to boot, outside the men's room. Second, the notion of Italians in the basement is by now proverbial and archetypical; we all remember, for instance, the history of the Italian language mass celebrated in the basement of churches run by the Irish. Third, against the more usual lore of bringing the important discussions to the kitchen, here, Louis brings an "important" conversation to the toilet, which, in turn, questions the significance of the topic at hand as well as Louis's lack of respect for Black and Blue.[8] In the end, Louis does not show up. In so doing,

---

[8] It is of common opinion that the kitchen is, according to Lara Pascali, the "social center of the home... where Italian women typically prepare food, families gather for dinner, entertain guests, and celebrate holidays" (49). While not part of my discussion, Pascali goes on

Louis has totally dismissed Black and Blue as interlocutors with respect to the business item at hand. Further still, his disdain is such that he has them killed, literally, in the toilet, something planned well in advance, as we find out in the brief car scene with Louis and Roloff:

> ROLOFF: I could have taken care of this out in Queens. Look at
> the mess you have now.
> LOUIS: My son can handle it.

At this point in the film, the inference can only be that Louis had already planned the entire evening. In having done so, he now figures as the puppeteer — I purposefully reference here the iconoclastic, visual referent we first saw on the book jacket of the first edition of Mario Puzo's famous novel, *The Godfather* (1969 — or, better still, the "Godfather" that he truly is throughout this narrative. Hence, Udo's sarcastic reference to Louis's table as the "Godfather's table" at the beginning of the movie now comes full circle as the accurate referent it was, from a semiotic viewpoint unbeknownst to us at that moment. Only now, in retrospect, does it acquire this meaning as well.[9]

What also becomes important at this juncture is that the fundamental, basic evaluative process that we witness through the actual assassination is anticipated by Paolo's use of Italian at this point; he turns to Carmen and states, "Vado a pisciare." A reference at this juncture to such a basic discharging of bodily waste is not, I would contend, a casual coincidence. Further still, the choreography of switching scenes back and forth — not dissimilar to the inimitable baptism scene in *The Godfather* (1972) — adds to the possible, if not probable, interpretant of a condemnation of organized crime, Carmen and Paolo's attempt to muscle Louis out of his restaurant in addition to the book-making business. Once Pao-

---

to underscore the importance of the kitchen in the basement, especially after World War II in areas around Toronto, Montreal, and New York.

[9] On the semiotics of retrospective reading, see my essay on the retro-lector (Tamburri 1990).

lo enters the bathroom, he finds Ken Roloff, the most affable Wall Streeter we previously met at the bar. But we find out at this moment that he is also a contract killer. Roloff's assassination of Paolo, especially, with the latter urinating into the toilet, brings together two forms of waste that need to be eliminated if not eradicated: the murderer Paolo and bodily waste. Indeed, Paolo falls between the toilet bowl and the urinal, with his last word, to Carmen, having been the above-mentioned "pisciare," a three-syllable word in Italian whose first two syllables afford greater emphasis on the bodily waste than the English monosyllabic infinitive "piss." Italian, thus, or one's knowledge of Italian, is potentially more fulfilling (pun intended) with regard to the spectator's greater understanding of the above-mentioned nuances of the situation at hand; the linguistic enhances the visual and the contextual, which together create a greater semiotic interpretant.

As the assassination takes place the montage is as follows. As soon as Paolo falls covered in blood between the toilet and the urinal, the scene switches to the kitchen where the cooks meticulously prepare the many of the 263 dinners the restaurant will end up serving by evening's end. Roloff then turns toward Carmen and shoots him. Likewise, as he falls, the scene switches back to kitchen as well. All of this is in a slightly slowed down projection, as if to be sure, among other things, that these two diametrically opposed scenes stand out. The newness of Udo's cuisine and all that it pertains now overshadows the murder of Paolo and Carmen, two small-town criminals who, to this moment, lived according to old-school criminality often associated with Italian Americans. To top it off, once Carmen falls to his death, the switching of scenes this time is no longer to the kitchen. Instead, we see a group of customers applauding after which there is an immediate switch to Carmen who definitively falls to his death at the bottom of the stairwell. All this as soon as Paolo's headfirst hit the mirror once he is shot by Roloff, and the entire scene is accompanied by the pop song "Oh what a night!" Such a sequence surely figures in its own right as, in general, a condemnation of the "old world," as it does, in particular, a condemnation of Carmen and Paolo and their bullish behavior.[10] Hence, in the end, Udo nouveau Italian cuisine is highlighted in the positive while the murderous bullying behavior of the small-town organized criminals is stamped out once and for all. The potential semiotics of it all at this juncture should be most apparent.

IDENTITY

As I have already discussed in the previous chapter, Daniel Aaron, Rose Basile Green, Irvin Child, and Charles Sanders Peirce together constitute the requisite theoretical arsenal to consider Italian/American identity through a different lens. More germane to our discussion of *Dinner Rush*, the notions of Child and Peirce come into play in a manner similar to what we saw in the previous chapter on *Big Night* with regard to Primo, Secondo, and Pascal. This time our trio is Louis, Duncan, and Udo.

That said, in *Dinner Rush* we witness once more the three types of Italian Americans that constitute the previously mentioned progression in the previous chapter from a stage of visceral allegiance to national identity with passage through that secondary stage of the "apathetic." In the end, then, as we concluded in the previous chapter on *Big Night*, we have three distinct phenomena of identity: (1) a strong allegiance to national origins; (2) in down-playing a strong allegiance, the desire to amalgamate one's culture of origin with the host culture—indeed, reconcile the differences between them; and (3) further still, an unmitigated, *sui generis* adherence to the host culture. Thus, as we had seen with Primo, Secondo, and Pascal, here now we have Louis, Duncan, and Udo, as a new trinity of representation of these three identitarian phenomena.

At this juncture, one may wonder about the inclusion of Duncan in this paradigm. After all, he is not Italian, and this we can assume by (1) the music that accompanies him, and (2) his own use of Spanish, however rare. Nonetheless, the shifting definitions of "Italian" cuisine and, we must not forget, of "Italian" cooks, allows us to step

---

[10] This is not dissimilar to my analysis of Michael Corleone's tie as I discussed in a previous venue (Tamburri 2011, 80-91).

beyond the traditional conceptualizations of what the adjective Italian now can, and might very well, signify. Louis, already at the beginning of the film, questioned the definition of "Italian" as in restaurant and cuisine when he rhetorically stated for that moment in the film, "Of course, why would there be Italians in an Italian kitchen?" However, re-considering this question now at the end of the film when he meets Harold for the first time, we might now re-conceptualize what we mean by Italian and, hence, by Italian identity. Louis asks, "Are you new here?" Harold responds, "Yes." But he also states that he is not Italian, to which Louis laughs and says, "You can't have everything." Well, perhaps we can.

In an essay of mine in the collection *Re-Mapping Italian America*, I address the notion of a re-conceptualization of the definition of the adjective Italian in reference to the idea of the "Italian" writer. My premise is one based on the notion of an identity being defined not by one's familial heritage and/or geographical provenance but instead by one's socio-behavioral and cultural experience; namely, her/his daily activities in life vis-à-vis those things that fall squarely within the realm of "a largely Italian milieu, and not necessarily only in Italy" (Tamburri 2017, 67). As such, it thus "unfolds in that way specifically because s/he feels [it] as part of his/her ordinary existence, and not in any honorary or affected sense, but actually *effective*" (Tamburri 2017, 67).

As I did then, I shall cite here once more what Rebecca West wrote thirty years ago about a concept of Italian and/or Italian/American identity, of someone who is not of Italian origin but who lives out his/her daily activities—be they professional or personal—if not specifically within, then at least for the most part close to what is coming to be called *italianità*, or s/he lives her daily life *italianamente*:

By bringing non-Italian or Italian/American perspectives to Italian literature and culture [...], we implicitly (and at times explicitly) question essentialist views of ethnicity. I could go so far as to say that I am, by dint of twenty-five years of study, scholarship, and professional engagement in Italian culture and literature, a kind of "Italian/American" (or "American/Italian"). This identity is not to be found in my genes, my blood, or in any part of my material body, but rather in my orientation, my knowledge, and my commitment. [...] Similarly, adopted cultures may be seen in the same light as adopted children. If those children are more truly the children of their adoptive parents who nurture and cherish them than of their biological parents, then perhaps an adopted culture is eventually as much (or in some cases even more) "mine" as it is that of someone born into it. I recognize that I may never "feel" Italian or Italian/American in the same way that natural sons and daughters of Italian culture may feel, but I would at the very least like to believe that my investment in that culture has marked me more than superficially as someone who is part of *italianità*." (337)

If we accept the basic premise of what West is saying, that she in some way—and maybe on the strength of "twenty-five years of study, research, and responsibilities having to do with Italian culture and literature," belongs within the rather vast confines of *italianità*, we must then include in this world of *italianità* not only also those who, while born and raised in Italy, live elsewhere, and in our case, in the United States, but we then should also include those who, while not born into an ethnicity, possess nevertheless an orientation and knowledge of, as well as a commitment to, all things Italian and to which they pertain.[11] Indeed, I would submit that we can do so quite easily from a scientific point of view if we are willing to break free from those arbitrary, and dare I say, limiting confines. In so doing, we thus recognize that kaleidoscopic mosaic that is North America, as I classified it more than twenty-five years ago,[12] and what now resonates in what Michele Cometa states in his *Studi culturali* with regard to the "migrant" writer: "The mosaic of

---

[11] If we enlarge further this concept of West's, we find ourselves in the end converging with the concept of "Italicity," which Piero Bassetti has been promulgating since 2002 and which he elaborated in (2008).

[12] I addressed it for the first time in my *To Hyphenate* (1991) 48-51, and later in my *Una semiotica* (2010) 62-64.

identities that migrant writers carry around with them is much more complex and variegated" (107), which is also true, as we have seen above, even in the case of someone like West. Following, then, such an intellectual trajectory with regard to migrant writers, writers of other limitations, and/or of ethnic ones, we can only end up colliding — and happily so — with the Bassettian discourse of "italici" and, in the broader sense of the concept of "Italian" identity, we thus find ourselves in an "Italian" world that surpasses every restrictive, reductive, and essentialist conceptual barrier. This, ultimately, I would submit, should be our end goal in our continued endeavors to change paradigms.

Now, with this as a conceptual backdrop, we can readily understand how, within this filmic world of *Dinner Rush*, Duncan is very much part of the "Italian" milieu of Gigino's restaurant, which constitutes our semiosphere as viewers — that space within which sign processes operate and outside of which semiosis cannot take place. As viewers, that is, we are engaged in the textual world of the film we are watching. Hence, and in like fashion, for Duncan, his world is the world of Gigino's, an Italian restaurant owned and operated by "Italians."

Thus, in re-visiting Child's three stages, it becomes clear that Duncan — the Italian social construct that he now is — finds himself situated literally between Louis and Udo. In such a position, and given what we have seen, he surely manifests the apathetic reaction. There are two episodes we have already witnessed, each of which underscores his desire, on the one hand, to "please his [cohort Italian Americans such as Louis]" — i.e., his preparation of Louis's sausage and peppers dish — and, on the other hand, to gain acceptance and recognition from Udo — i.e., his co-preparation of the special lobster dish for the food critic Jennifer Freely. Duncan thus inhabits that middle space of Child's apathetic reaction between Louis the "in-grouper" and Udo the "rebel."

That said, then, "[i]n our post-structuralist world of all sorts of borders having been readily traversed, diminished[, if not completely eliminated, and all sorts of concepts and terminology redefined], this [notion of a] new 'Italian' ... allows for a more profound understanding of the current situation at hand, as well as for a more fertile field of study of the trans-national discourse in which Italians engage but that, from a hegemonic point of view, do not [always] recognize. The insistence on a limited and, dare I say, limiting [notion of what it means to be 'Italian'] restricted to Italy-born and bred can only stifle the critical voice that wishes to make the evident connections that indeed exist under a more broad umbrella that we can still—and, I would underscore, *should* —readily call "Italian" (Tamburri 2017, 75).

WORKS CITED

Bassetti, Piero. 2008. *Italici. Il possibile futuro di una community globale*. Milano: Casagrande, 2008.

_____. 2002. "Italicity: Global and Local", in *The Essence of Italian Culture and the Challenge of a Global Age*, edited by Paulo Ianni and George F. McLean. Washington, DC: The Council for Research in Values and Philosophy. 13-24.

Bell, David and Gill Valentine, eds. 1997. *Consuming Geographies: We Are Where We Eat*. London: Routledge.

Calabretta-Sadjer, Ryan. 2018. "The Bargaining Performative and Awakening Potential of Foodways in Bob Giraldi's *Dinner Rush,*" *Journal of Popular Film and Television* 46.4. 195-206.

Campisi, Paul. 1948. "Ethnic Family Patterns: The Italian Family in the United States," *The American Journal of Sociology* 53.6 (May).

Child, Irvin L. 1943. *Italian or American? The Second Generation in Conflict*. New Haven: Yale University Press.

Cinotto, Simone. 2013. *The Italian American Table. Food, Family, and Community in New York City*. Champaign, IL: University of Illinois Press.

Cometa, Michele. 2010. *Studi culturali*. Napoli: Guida.

Dinner Rush. 2000. Dir. Bob Giraldi. Access Motion Picture Group, Giraldi-Suarez-DiGiamo Productions. 1h 39 min. Released 29 March 2002 (UK).

Ferry, Jane F. 2003. *Food in Film: A Culinary Performance of Communication*. New York: Routledge.

Green, Rose Basile. 1974. *The Italian-American Novel: A Document of the Interaction of Two Cultures*. Madison, NJ: Fairleigh Dickinson University Press.

ISSNAF. Italian Scientists and Scholars in North America Foundation. http://www.issnaf.org/about-us/mission.html.

Keller, James R. 2006. "Filming and Eating Italian: *Big Night* and *Dinner Rush.*" In *Food, Film And Culture: A Genre Study.* Jefferson, N.C.: McFarland & Co.

Lindenfeld, Laura and Fabio Parasecoli. 2016. *Feasting Our Eyes: Food Films and Cultural Identity in the United States.* New York: Columbia University Press. For *Dinner Rush*, 48-51.

Lopreato, Joseph. 1970. *Italian Americans.* New York: Random House.

_____. 1967. *Peasants No More: Social Class and Social Change in an Underdeveloped Society.* San Francisco: Chandler Publishing Co.

Lyotard, Francois. 1984 (1979). The Postmodern Condition: A Report on Knowledge. Trans. Geoff Bennington and Brian Massumi. Foreword by Fredric Jameson. Minneapolis: University of Minnosota Press.

Merrell, Floyd. 1991. *Signs Becoming Signs: Our Perfusive, Pervasive Universe.* Bloomington: Indiana University Press.

Peirce, Charles Sanders. 1960. *Principles of Philosophy* in *Collected Papers,* eds., Charles Hartshorne and Paul Weiss, Vol. 1. Cambridge, MA: Harvard University Press.

Puzo, Mario. 1969. *The Godfather.* New York: Putnam.

Ruberto, Laura E. 2003. "Where Did the Goodfellas Learn to Cook? Gender, Labor, and the Italian American Experience." *Italian Americana* 21.2 (Summer): 164-76.

Ruberto, Laura and Joseph Sciorra. 2017a. "Introduction" in *New Italian Migrations to the United States. Vol. 1: Politics and History since 1945.* Champaign, IL: University of Illinois Press.

Scapp, Ron and Brian Seitz, editors. 1998. *Eating Culture.* Albany: SUNY Press.

Singer, June. 1976. *Androgyny. Toward a New Theory of Sexuality.* New York: Anchor Press.

Tamburri, Anthony Julian. 2017. "The Coincidence of Italian Cultural Hegemonic Privilege and the Historical Amnesia of Italian Diaspora Articulations" in *Re-Mapping Italian America. Places, Cultures, Identity,* Sabrina Vellucci and Carla Francellini, eds. New York: Bordighera Press. 53-76.

_____. 2015. "Viewing *Big Night* as Easy as One, Two, Three: A Triadic Notion of an Italian/American Identity." *Luci e ombre* 3.2.

_____. 2011. *Re-viewing Italian Americana: Generalities and Specificities on Cinema.* New York: Bordighera Press.

_____. 2010. *Una semiotica dell'etnicità. Nuove segnalature per la scrittura italiano/americana.* Franco Cesati Editore.

_____. 2003. *Semiotics of Re-reading: Guido Gozzano, Aldo Palazzeschi, and Italo Calvino.* Madison, NJ: Fairleigh Dickinson UP.

_____. 1990. "Aldo Palazzeschi's *:riflessi.* Toward a Notion of a 'Retro-Lector'." *The American Journal of Semiotics.* 7.1/2: 105-24.

West, Rebecca. 1991. "Scorsese's *Who's That Knocking At My Door?* Night Thoughts on Italian Studies in the United States." *Romance Languages Annual.* Ben Lawton and Anthony Julian Tamburri, eds. 331-338.

Signing Italian/American Cinema,
Code-switching in the City:
What Does Scorsese Mean in *Mean Streets*?

PRELIMINARY THOUGHTS

The Telluride Film Festival in 1994 had, at the time, a section dedicated to the "student director." This usually included graduates of the various MA/MFA programs in filmmaking. As some may know, Florida State University has one of the best undergraduate BFA programs in filmmaking; and that year Joseph Greco, a newly minted BFA graduate from FSU, had his thesis accepted by the Telluride Film Festival, curiously entitled *Lena's Spaghetti*.[1]

I watched the film with much interest; after all, I was already five years into the creation of the educational entity, Bordighera Incorporated, and its future imprint Bordighera Press, with Paolo Giordano and Fred Gardaphé. A goodly part of our mission was to uncover, so to speak, those Italian/American cultural artists and artisans who, for reasons sometimes inexplicable, were not recognized as such, or, worse still, their work was oddly discounted because it dealt too much with Italian themes — excluding, of course, those works dedicated to organized crime. So, you might imagine, a film entitled *Lena's Spaghetti* by someone named Joseph Greco could only arouse great interest.

The people I was with thought it was very aptly done; though, except for the title, they could not for the life of them see how it had anything to do with Italians. Not wanting to dismiss the film outright, I later asked Greco if he would send me a VHS, promising that I would write a review for our journal *Voices in Italian Americana*. He did, and I did not. That is, I did not write a typical review.

---

[1] To date, Joseph Greco has completed one feature-length film based on his own experiences as a young man. *Canvas* (Canvas Pictures, 2008) is the story of an Italian/American couple (Mary [Marcia Gay Hardin] and John [Joe Pantoliano] Marino) struggling with the wife's schizophrenia, seen through the perspective of their young son (Chris [Devon Gearhart]).

What I did do was write a review essay that later went on to become part of a small book on Italian/American short films (Tamburri 2002). That essay was entitled, "Subliminal Ethnicity: What is [~~not~~] Italian/American about *Lena's Spaghetti?*" The title of that essay begged a couple of questions, to be sure, one of which I had already dealt with elsewhere—a re-definition of Italian/American art forms from a post-1950s perspective: post-1950s not just for the advent of new ideas, rather a time when the notion of exploring new ideas achieved some sort of validity. I make this distinction because while there were new faces on the scene, older faces, often forgotten by the establishment, were revived, re-read, and re-appropriated for constructing a different critical discourse.[2] Other questions that arose were: "Why is 'not' under erasure?" and, "What can I possibly mean by 'subliminal'?"

Both of these questions are related; and suffice it to say that I used the adjective "subliminal" precisely because of its ambiguity—an ambiguity that carries the various definitions of: (1) barely perceptible, (2) inadequate to produce a sensation or a perception, or (3) existing or functioning outside the area of conscious awareness. All three definitions echo in some form or another Victor Turner's well-known and well-cited definition of liminal entities as being "necessarily ambiguous [...]"; they are, as Turner continues, "neither here nor there; they are betwixt and between the positions assigned and arrayed by law, custom, convention, and ceremonial" (Turner, 95-100).

MEAN STREETS: THE INFORMED ITALIAN/AMERICAN SPECTATOR

These questions of more than twenty-five years ago remain equally significant today as we move forward in Italian/American studies, be our critical performance dedicated to the already known artists or to those whose works (1) have fallen by the wayside, or, (2) not adhering to a dominant cultural notion of what is Italian/Amer-

---

[2] My own re-reading of Italian/American literature appropriates the newer voices such as Umberto Eco, Hans-Georg Gadamer, Wolfgang Iser, etc.; yet it also goes back to C. S. Peirce, whose seminal notions of the sign—firstness, secondness, thirdness—lie at the base of my 1994 essay.

ican, have not garnered the requisite attention to be part of a dominant cultural discourse. Hence, the above-mentioned notions of ambiguity and subliminality can continue to enhance our readings and viewings today as they did with *Lena's Spaghetti*.[3] In this regard, then, my essay interrogates the various possibilities of signification that emanate from Martin Scorsese's *Mean Streets* (1973). It especially examines his use of signage, both literal and metaphorical, in creating a situation for potential polyvalence that is dependent on his spectator's cultural reservoir.

The problematics of Scorsese's films vis-à-vis their viewers had already been underscored in the 1980s by Philip Kolker, who saw in the director's films, and with particular regard to *Mean Streets*, "a tension between the viewer's expectations and desires to be comfortably situated within the narrative and ... the stubborn refusal of the narrative to meet those expectations and desires" (170). Of course, such a statement, as keen as it may seem, calls into question the notion of expectations and what they are supposed to be, if we can even speak in these terms today, given the plethora of critical tools available to us. Said "tension," or complication, was further referenced a few years later as "fragmentation in point of view" by Les Keyser, due to, as he stated, "the opening sequences, when real home movies of the Scorsese family gradually open up to the larger movie of Charlie's current life. Then Charlie goes to the mirror to assess his own reflection, only to stumble back (in a triple cut) to his own bed. Within minutes complex narrative issues have been raised: What is real and what is dream? Which side of the mirror will this film focus on? How do these home movies relate to the commercial film at hand? And why is reality being restructured and by whom?" (45-46).

---

[3] My analysis of *Lena's Spaghetti* spoke to the value of secondary and tertiary signs that, at first glance, seemed to possess little signifying value with regard to Italian Americanness. Such signs, for example, included postcards with the proverbial Renaissance putti, which Lena and Herbie exchanged; Herbie's painting of Lena, which recalls the classic photo of Sophia Loren eating spaghetti in an Italian restaurant in 1953 (photo by Franco Fedel); the name of Herbie's colleague/flirtation, Adele; Herbie's inviting Adele to Italian dinner.

Both Kolker and Keyser are speaking to the challenges of interpretation and how queries of, if not for, signification can, on the one
hand, be daunting, leaving us with more questions than before. Or,
on the other hand, such inquiries can prove constitutive, leading
the viewer, in our case, to a more broadened field of signification.
This second case, I would submit, does not necessarily cancel out
what we might call the less transcendent results of meaning making; indeed, I would suggest, it adds to a greater potentiality of signification that the text and its plethora of signs might ultimately
produce. That said, then, Scorsese's Italian/American films have
much to offer the informed spectator, that individual who is notably experienced in film criticism and may very well unpack *Mean
Streets* and thus demonstrate the potential in signification that the
film offers. Yet, I would go one step further, especially with regard
to these "ethnic" films of his, as we are apt to label them, and contend that Scorsese's informed, *Italian/American* spectator may actually have access, to be sure, to a greater inventory of meaning. My
use of the term "Italian/American spectator" is not grounded in
biology. I am not limiting my referents to those who are genetically
Italian. I wish to expand my use of the term here as I have done
elsewhere.[4] There, I spoke in terms of an *"effective identity …* in as
much as it recognizes the quality of everyday activity in which the
individual lives out his/her daily life; an *effective identity* also insofar as it recognizes that what an individual does within a largely
Italian milieu unfolds in that way specifically because that person
feels his/her actions to be done 'Italian-ly' — *italianamente* we would
say in Italian — as part of his/her ordinary existence, and not in any
honorary or *affected* sense, but actually 'effective,' such that whatever s/he does — and that s/he knows, as an Italian would — is part of
the every-day life of that person. And so, that 'Italian effect' of his/

---

[4] See Tamburri (2015). I am converging here with the concept of "Italicity," which Piero
Bassetti has been promulgating since 2002. He further elaborated his concept in 2008, and
finally in 2015. In specifics, I mentioned Ben Lawton and Rebecca West (2014, 139) and
Rebecca West and Jhumpa Lahiri (2017) as examples of those individuals who, not somati-
cally Italian, have acquired an Italian culture equal to if not greater than many who are in
fact genetically Italian.

her daily life is precisely that blending of Italian characteristics and /or *Italianistic-ness* of his/her identity" (Tamburri 2014: 135). It is, I went on to say, "a concept of Italian and/or Italian/American identity, of someone who is not by ethnic origin Italian, but who lives out her/his daily activities, be they professional or personal, if not specifically within, then at least for the most part close to what is coming to be called *Italianità*" (135-36). That said, then, in an attempt to identify some of Scorsese's imagistic acrobatics in light of his informed "Italian/American" spectator's familiarity with certain "Italian" signs, the film indeed affords this second type of informed spectator the privilege of greater signification.

For the complication of meaning production in general, let us look at a scene that, as far as I can tell, no one has readily addressed, especially with regard to the notion of a lack of direction and a sense of randomness that these characters manifest.[5] Indeed, the bar in which our *vitelloni* hang out is often crowded with a notable number of twenty- and thirty-somethings, mostly unaccompanied by anyone whom we might consider a significant other, a partner, or someone similar.[6] While often together in the bar, they are for all practical purposes alone within a crowd. This becomes apparent, I would suggest, when Johnny Boy enters the bar with his two "girlfriends." In this scene, the notion of partnered or not partnered, is indeed problematized in a couple of ways. First, we have the seemingly coupled, or, we might say, potentially coupled Johnny Boy

---

[5] Phillip Kolker wants to distinguish Tony the bar owner in this regard. He states the following: "But then none of the characters in the film, with the possible exception of Tony, the barkeeper, has the center or sense of direction that one expects from characters in conventional film fictions, and it is the purpose of the film to observe them in their randomness and as part of an unpredictable flow of events" (168).

[6] Peter Bondanella reminds us of Scorsese's own admission of Fellini's influence on Scorsese in making this film: "By Scorsese's own testimony in his four-hour documentary *Il mio viaggio in Italia*, *Mean Streets* owes a great debt to the model of Federico Fellini's *I vitelloni* (1953, *The Vitelloni*), a coming-of-age film that follows five slackers around their provincial city on the Adriatic coast of Italy. Fellini's adolescents growing up in the 1950s, however, lack the violent edge, the profanity, the rage, the immorality, and the close association with the underworld that characterize Scorsese's citizens of Little Italy. Fellini's nostalgic view of his youth also avoids the brand of Italian American Catholicism and the particular brand of Catholic guilt that marks Scorsese's film as a work of art created by a man who once attended a seminary and considered becoming a priest" (79-80).

and his two girlfriends, one of whom, we soon find out, is for Charlie. But coupled they are not. Instead, all four, as is obvious, have randomly met, Johnny Boy having picked them up at the Greenwich Village, "bohemian" bar, Café Bizarre, and Charlie now meeting them here for the first time at Tony's.

They are strangers to each other, sentimentally unfulfilled and in search of some form of company that may, at least for the time being, attenuate their emotional deprivation. But, in reality, the scene is void of such a message; it underscores, to be sure, the very vacuous emotional state of the majority of the people who populate Tony's bar.[7] And while Charlie, Johnny Boy, Michael, and others we come to meet are indeed the main characters in this regard, this message of absence of emotional capital is punctuated for sure by the presence of the woman at the bar.

In her only appearance in *Mean Streets*, this woman incarnates the very state of loneliness. Seated at the end of the bar, she occupies a physical location away from the rest; except, we note, that she is right behind Charlie and staring straight ahead. As the camera moves in on Charlie, he eventually blocks our vision totally of her, for a second, as he lifts his glass to his mouth. It is not difficult to assume, especially in hindsight, that Charlie and she momentarily become one, together now as contributors to the potential significability of this scene. Having finished his drink, as we continue to view this scene, Charlie walks back around our woman at the bar and we, as viewers, now have a full portrait of this woman, static as she is, staring still into space, as just mentioned, but this time, a bit downward. Her solo portrait, all alone at the end of the bar, and as brief as it may be, punctuates, I contend, the visual paradox of this entire scene. Namely, in this bar full of people, and specifically Johnny Boy with his two newly met girlfriends, it is nothing more

---

[7] In quoting Robert Casillo, Jonathan Cavallero wants to discount Kolker's "cinema of loneliness" and substitute it with "a cinema of group solidarity'": "[M]any of [Scorsese's] films that focus on Italian American characters might be more accurately described as 'a cinema of group solidarity'" (Cavallero, 46). Perhaps, but it is also true that these characters are, emotionally speaking, loners who are unable to connect with others in any sort of productive manner.

than a gathering place for all the lonely people, as physical satisfaction and not emotional fulfillment is the order of the evening. Indeed, the projection of our female's gaze moves from straight ahead to downward, as just noted, and is a gesture that may readily signal greater dejection of the situation at hand.

There is another aspect of this scene that proves significant. Once Johnny Boy and the two women begin their walk the length of the bar, on their way to join up with Charlie, the timing of the action is slightly slowed down, beginning with Charlie. As Johnny Boy finishes putting his pants back on, the camera switches to us watching Charlie, who is obviously watching Johnny Boy. It is thus from Johnny Boy's perspective that this scene opens; and it is in a slightly slow-motion perspective, until the camera's movement closes in on Charlie whose full portrait blocks out the single woman at the bar thus merging the two, as mentioned above. Then, suddenly, the perspective changes, and we are now watching Johnny Boy and his two female friends walking down the bar. Thus, too, is in slow motion. However, at midpoint the camera switches to Tony who, smiling while watching the threesome move along, is filmed in regular time. As mentioned earlier, Tony is the only one of the mail characters in *Mean Streets* who has a "center or sense of direction that one expects from characters in conventional film fictions," to quote Kolker once more. Hence, Tony's portrayal here is communicated in regular time.

The slow-motion effect here has the clear objective of making us notice the machinations of the scene as we are prompted by Charlie's thoughts. Johnny Boy is Charlie's penance, as he thinks out loud, and we, as spectators, are now put on notice. And just in case we missed the cue form Charlie's thoughts, such a warning is inherent in the opening words of the song "Jumpin' Jack Flash," as we hear "1, 2"—their cue to start walking and ours to take heed—just before Johnny Boy and his two new female friends begin to make their way down the bar. As they do, and as the song continues:

I was born in a crossfire hurricane. / And I howled at the maw in the drivin' range. / But it's all right now. / In fact, it's a gas. / But it's all right. / Jumpin' Jack Flash. / It's a gas, gas, gas!

These words seem to constitute an uncanny parallel to Johnny Boy, whom we have briefly witnessed thus far and what we shall witness later on. For the most part, he is a contrarian to all that is good, decorous, and responsible. Further still, everything he does has no goal other than an immediate result whatever it may be. Hence, born in a "crossfire hurricane" signals his chaotic origins, and "howl[ing] at the maw" underscores (a) his recklessness in the face of danger, and, by extension, (b) his desire to ignore all that might smack of rules and regulations. In the end, then, the only thing to do—"But it's all right"—is to engage in that behavior that brings pleasure—"In fact, it's a gas."—whatever that pleasure might be.

CODE-SWITCHING

In his book, *Hollywood's Italian American Filmmakers: Capra, Scorsese, Savoca, Coppola, and Tarantino*, Jonathan Cavallero stated the following in his chapter dedicated to Martin Scorsese:

Those of us who grew up outside of these communities or do not or cannot claim Italian heritage can use our ethnic or class standings or both as a way of distancing ourselves from the characters and their exclusionary thinking. (Cavallero, 65)

I would state, instead, the following: Those of us who grew up inside these communities—or, as non-somatically Italian, who have become notably familiar with the socio-cultural phenomena of said communities—can use our ethnic understanding and/or class standings, or both, as a way of interrogating further the characters and their ethnic thinking and behavior. Case in point being the scene that immediately follows Johnny Boy's long walk down the bar, eventually to meet up with Charlie.

There are two elements in this scene, I would submit, that could readily escape the non-Italian/American spectator, both of which are linguistic. As to the relevance of language, and here specifically Italian, we are given a cue when Johnny Boy and Charlie come together and hug each other, as Italian (read, also, Italian American) men regularly do. The cue, as we saw above, is that Charlie greets Johnny Boy and addresses him as "Giovannino," literally, "little Johnny," or, as we know him, Johnny Boy. We are thus, once more, put on notice that Italian, this time, might play some role as we move forward. Indeed, as we shall see, it does. So, before continuing, however, we need to remember that the two women whom Johnny Boy picked up are named Sarah Klein and Heather Weintraub, two Jewish women one might presume from their names, who were hanging out at the "bohemian" bar, as Tony classifies it.[8]

In tune with the paradoxical situation of visuality mentioned earlier, we find at this juncture an analogous contradiction of terms. When Charlie decides to address Johnny Boy in more formal and, dare we say, respectful terms, he calls him by his last name, as we heard. The pronunciation is ambiguous, to be sure. While some may understand his last name to be "Civello" here, as we listen closely, instead, we can actually hear, pronounced in English, the word "cervello," the Italian term for "brains." And it is in this vein that the paradox comes to life; Johnny Boy has proven to be anything but "smart" (read, "brainy") as he has racked up an inordinate amount of debt, going from one loan shark to another in order to borrow money. This exceedingly impetuous behavior that is by all means self-destructive, is accompanied by a violent streak that can also result in actions at the expense of others. I have in mind here the opening scene of our introduction to Johnny Boy, when, for reasons only he knows, he blows up the mailbox, apparently unconcerned for those who might be in the line of fire of the shrapnel. Thus, "cervello" he is not. Instead, he exudes what we have seen to understand as a clearly violent, irre-

---

[8] There is an extra-filmic fact that proves curious indeed with the names. First, the aforementioned Jewish aspect; second, Martin Scorsese's lover at the time was named "Sandy Weintraub [and she] had an enormous input in the rewriting" (Keyser 37). Dare we then assume that the emphasis that Johnny Boy places on Heather's name is, in some sense, a homage to Sandy? Just a thought.

sponsible mindset for which he demonstrates an absolute callous attitude for those around him. Hence, the paradox of Mr. Cervello —Mr. Brains—is manifested by his erratic behavior that is totally contrary to what we might expect from any semblance of a *brainy* person.[9]

The second aspect of this scene that falls into the same category of the aforementioned characteristics of being barely perceptible or, for the non-Italian/American informed spectator, existing or functioning outside the area of ethnic conscious awareness. It, too, has a linguistic foundation. It speaks to the biases and prejudices that may very well exist within this community, which here are manifested by and articulated in a language that is not by any means the *lingua franca* of the bar, especially of those who are not Italian American. Rather, Charlie uses a pidgin form of Italian in his directions to Tony when he states: "Tony, give the, ahhh, 'mazzacrist' whatever they want." Like the appearance of the woman at the bar, this sentence is a *seemingly* insignificant articulation that, under the guise of generosity—"Give the [women] whatever they want."— actually carries a more potent meaning and hence communicates, again paradoxically, Charlie's negative opinion of these two women and their ethnic/cultural heritage. As if to say, "Sure, we'll be generous here, but they are, after all, Christ-killers, let's not forget." Otherwise, there is no reason for Charlie to refer to them as 'mazzacrist'. In fact, they are,—we find out after the back-room conversation between Charlie and Johnny Boy—nothing more than sexual objects for our two men. In the end, then, they are totally dehumanized both religiously and sexually.

Such ethnic degradation, we know, is not limited to Jews in *Mean Streets*. Charlie's infatuation with the dancer Diane, an attractive African/American woman, is thwarted precisely because she is

---

[9] There may indeed be those who want to see a different side of Johnny Boy since, when on the roof with a gun in his hand, he does display some acknowledgement of what he is doing is off base. I have in mind his apology, so to speak, to the anonymous woman whose window his gunshot broke. It is not the apology that is telling, it is the fact that he engages in such behavior of random shooting that underscores his socio-pathology of no concern for others. The apology, in the end, has no real value; after all, the damage is already done.

black. According to such tribalistic modes of thinking, Diane loses out because (1) she is not Italian, a primary rule according to old-world thinking, and, most horridly from Charlie's perspective, (2) she is black. There is the Italian expression, "Moglie e buoi dei paesi tuoi!" The meaning of this pithy phrase urges loyalty to local customs and hence underscores, for sure, diffidence to foreigners. Here, of course, it is complicated by the difference in race between Diane and Charlie. A difference, we come to understand, as we are privy to Charlie's thoughts:

> Y' know.... she's really good-looking ... really good-looking.
> I've gotta say that again. She's really good looking ... but she's
>   black.... You can see that real plain.
> When you get down to it though ... there's not much of a differ-
>   ence, is there?
> Well ... is there?

Of course, there is no answer. Let us, however, remember that Charlie has truly privileged Diane here, as there are two dancers on stage, both "good-looking," to use Charlie's words: one is black, the other white. Charlie is clearly obsessed with Diane. But his desire is thwarted, as already mentioned, by the old-world customs of "sticking to your own" that is now problematized here for Charlie by Diane's race.

As with the two Jewish women, the eventual rejection here is also explained in pidgin Italian racist terminology. As Charlie approaches the place where he was to meet Diane, he tells the cabbie first to stop and then, changing his mind, he asks to be brought back to where the cabbie picked him up. Again, what is important here, for our case in point, is his adherence to old-world values complicated by racial and ethnic prejudices. Once more, we are privy to his thoughts; we hear the following: "Crazy... That's all I need now, is to get caught in the village with a melinjan." The term "melinjan" is equally offensive for blacks, as the above-cited "'mazzacrist'" is for Jews.

What Charlie ultimately does by using Italian words instead of their English equivalents is engage in classic code-switching. His use of "two ... linguistic varieties [here, English and Italian] in the same conversation" (Myers-Scotton and Ury 5) allows him, first and foremost, to create an exclusive group in so far as only his Italian/American friends—or those who are intimate with the language and culture—will grasp the nuance of the Italian terms. In so doing, he creates, further still, a type of power imbalance, as the two Jewish women, for instance, have absolutely no idea what the meaning of "mazzacrist" is, and thus remain ignorant of the biases that exist within this social situation and hence unaware of any potential consequences that may arise. Charlie has, in the end, moved the situation from what some call in code-switching the "identity arena," in his use of Italian with Johnny Boy and Tony, to the "power arena" in his use of a language, Italian, in front of those—here, Sarah Klein and Heather Weintraub—who do not understand it.[10]

In both cases Charlie has articulated two terms that could not —indeed, do not—have equally derogatory synonyms in Italian/ American speak; they are truly the *ne plus ultra* of negative offensive speak within Italian/American communities, which are articulated, we must underscore, in a type of pidgin Italian, and not simply an English slang we might associate with Italians in America. In this second case, still, there is the comparison to the vegetable world, one step further in denigration that literally dehumanizes the referent. The "'mazzacrist'" is still a human being albeit a sacrilegious one; the "moulinyan"—or "melinjan," as Charlie states —is reduced to an inanimate object. Hence, one's intimacy or lack thereof with Italian/American speak is fundamental to the specta-

---

[10] Myers-Scotton and Ury state the following in this regard: "[I]nteractions in these data can be defined in terms of the interchange within three social arenas: (1) *The identity arena*: Interactions within this arena depend on a degree of identity existing among participants. In terms of at least one factor, such as occupation or age grade, participants are members of the same group. Many interactions between family members or of the same ethnic group fall into this arena. (2) *The power arena*: Power relationships are always unequal. When one or more participants invokes a power differential between participants as a factor salient to the outcome of the interaction, then the interaction takes place in the power arena. (3) *The transactional arena*: Interactions in this arena may be defined negatively: they are neither within the identity arena nor within the power arena. Neither personal affinity nor relative personal power is salient" (9).

tors's ability, or lack thereof, to grasp the nuance of the vitriol of such terms, be that term an ethnic or a racial epithet of the type used by Charlie.

There is yet another complication by such linguistic vitriol. All of this is further problematized by the fact that Charlie is a devotee of St. Francis of Assisi, wanting to emulate the saint in every way, especially his notion of social action that he believed was Franciscan, as he stated to Teresa at the beach:

> "Who's going to help [Johnny Boy] if I don't? That's what's the matter.... Nobody tries to help people.... Francis of Assisi had it all down... He knew..."

To the Italian/American spectator, I would submit, the manifestations of Charlie's Franciscan paradox ring ever more loudly when set alongside such language as "'mazzacrist'" and "moulinyan." The fraternal benevolence of the saint is now juxtaposed to the linguistic violence of Italian/American speak that Charlie himself adopts with such ease, and the metaphoric clash could not clamor more loudly.

Italian language adds further intrigue to Tony's bar. Leaving aside now the classification of the bar as a sort of den of iniquity and, related to be sure, the use of color—especially the red tint through which we view everything—the name of Tony's bar, "Volpe," adds to further interpretive speculation. "Volpe" is the Italian word for "fox," which metaphorically can refer to a person as sly, clever, or even a bright spark, this last definition, in a non-humorous manner, of someone who is intelligent and full of energy and enthusiasm. We may indeed associate the bar's name to its owner. Tony is, after all, the only character of the four who seems to have some sense of direction and is grounded to a certain degree. We see this on a number of occasions, and especially toward the end of the film, when he sends off Charlie and Johnny Boy after the latter's threat to shoot Michael: "Get out of here before this really goes up.... [G]o to a movie first or something ... not good to be driving around right away. You know you can't do much for him now ... it's out of your hands." Here, once Johnny Boy has eliminated all possibility of his own redemption, Tony tells Charlie that his efforts are useless. More significant, however, is Tony's quasi anticipation of the final scene, as he tells Charlie that it's "not good to be driving around right away," as we soon thereafter realize.

Less involved with language per sé but relevant to our discussion of the Italian/American spectator is yet another scene where the local custom of gambling and bookmaking come together, as we often found in pre-state-run lottery Italian America. I have in mind one very brief scene: when Charlie enters his uncle's luncheonette early in the film. This seemingly insignificant scene has Charlie literally bracketed by two signs that advertise the legal New York State Lottery. Their presence can only contrast with the life his uncle is leading—gambling, loan sharking, etc.—which is also the one to which Charlie aspires. But that life is in danger of being eliminated, not only because it is illegal, but precisely because the state government had legalized the lottery a few years prior and, as such, would—and indeed had—eventually take over even the bookmaking of zio Giovanni and others. Namely, the New State Lottery has, in fact, squeezed out illegal bookmaking, which is anticipated here by the signs' bracketing of Charlie as he enters the luncheonette.

CONCLUSION(S), OF SORTS

What I have presented here is a series of scenes in *Mean Streets*, which, when viewed by those who grew up inside—or one most familiar with—an Italian/American community and its *sui generis* language similar to what we have seen here on screen, can surely interrogate further, and we might say differently to some extent, the sign system we perceive to be included therein. Our ethnic, Italian awareness—which includes language—and/or class standings, or both, can very well offer the Italian/American spectator a so-called enhanced way of seeing Italian America and its many facets in *Mean Streets*. In the end, we uncover an "other" type of viewer's relationship to the internal and external dynamics of Little Italy, as notions of race, gender, sexuality, friendship, companionship, family, and other issues come to the fore.

Given the notably problematic narrative structure of *Mean Streets*, as we have already seen above (Kolker, Keyser), we might consider borrowing from and paraphrasing Jean-François Lyotard as an appropriate way to close, for now. For if the film a director "produces [is] not in principle governed by pre-established rules [i.e., canon formation], and [it] cannot be judged according to a determining judgment, by applying familiar categories to [said film]" (81), then one may very well be able to look elsewhere for interpretive strategies. Precisely because, as Lyotard continues, "[t)hose rules and categories are what the work ... is looking for." We might then say that the filmmaker, as in Scorsese's case, is "working [not necessarily] without rules" but is adding to the already formulated set of rules and hence adds to the overall narrative reservoir established in part by the so-called "familiar categories" of a "determining judgment." That said, the informed Italian/American spectator, precisely because of his/her particular cultural reservoir, may very well be able to establish, as s/he proceeds, particular interpretive strategies "of what will have been [seen]." This special spectator, then, will proceed to recodify and reinterpret the seemingly arbitrary—that is, non-canonical—signs. Such an interpretive act relies on the individual's time and place, and in the case of *Mean Streets*; the time is the 1960s and 1970s, and the place is inner-city Little Italy. These, among other things, very well constitute the particular intertextual reservoir of the informed Italian/American spectator.

WORKS CITED

Bassetti, Piero. 2015. *Svegliamoci italici: manifesto per un future glocal.* Venice: Marsilio.

———. 2008. *Italici. Il possibile futuro di una community globale.* Milan: Casagrande.

———. 2002. *Challenge of a Global Age,* Paulo Ianni and George F. McLean, eds.; Washington, DC: The Council for Research in Values and Philosophy. 13-24.

Bondanella, Peter. 2004. *Hollywood Italians. Dagos, Palookas, Romeos, Wise Guys, and Sopranos.* New York: Continuum.

Casillo, Robert. 2006. *Gangster Priest: The Italian American Cinema of Mar-*

tin Scorsese. Toronto: University of Toronto Press, 2006.

Cavallero, Jonathan. 2011. *Hollywood's Italian American Filmmakers: Capra, Scorsese, Savoca, Coppola, and Tarantino*. Urbana-Champaign: University of Illinois Press.

Eco, Umberto. 1979. *The Role of the Reader: Explorations in the Semiotics of Texts*. Bloomington: Indiana University Press.

_____. 1976. *A Theory of Semiotics*. Bloomington: Indiana Indiana University Press.

Gadamer, Hans-Georg. 1988. *Truth and Method*. New York: Crossroad;

Iser, Wolfgang. 1978. *The Act of Reading. A Theory of Aesthetic Response*. Baltimore: Johns Hopkins University Press.

Keyser, Les. 1992. *Martin Scorsese*. New York: Twayne Publishers.

Kolker, Robert Phillip. 1988. *A Cinema of Loneliness. Penn, Kubrick, Scorsese, Spielberg, Altman*. New York: Oxford University Press, 2nd ed.

Lourdeaux, Lee. 1990. *Italian and Irish Filmmakers in America: Ford, Capra, Coppola, and Scorsese*. Philadelphia: Temple University Press.

LoBrutto, Vincent. 2008. *Martin Scorsese: A Biography*. Westport: Praeger.

Lyotard, Jean-François. 1984. *The Postmodern Condition: A Report on Knowledge*. Tr. Geoff Bennington and Brian Massumi with a foreword by Fredric Jameson. Minneapolis: University of Minnesota Press.

Mean Streets. 1973. Dr. Martin Scorsese. Warner Bros., Taplin-Perry-Scorsese. 1h 49min. Released 14 October.

Myers-Scotton, Carol and William Ury. 1977. "Bilingual Strategies: The Social Functions of Code-switching." *Journal of the Sociology of Language* 13: 5-20.

Peirce, Charles Sanders. 1960. *Collected Papers*, eds., Charles Hartshorne and Paul Weiss, Vol. 1. Cambridge, MA: Harvard University Press;

Tamburri, Anthony Julian. 2017. "The Coincidence of Italian Cultural Hegemonic Privilege and the Historical Amnesia of Italian Diaspora Articulations" in *Re-Mapping Italian America. Places, Cultures, Identity*. Sabrina Vellucci and Carla Francellini, eds. New York: Bordighera Press.

_____. 2015. "The "Italian" Writer: Reflections on a New Category" in *Transcending Borders, Bridging Gaps: Italian Americana, Diasporic Studies, and the University Curriculum*. Anthony Julian Tamburri and Fred Gardaphé, eds. New York: Calandra Institute. 135-42.

_____. 2014. *Re-reading Italian Americana: Generalities and Specificities on*

Literature and Criticism. Madison, NJ: Fairleigh Dickinson University Press.

_____. 2011. *Re-viewing Italian Americana: Generalities and Specificities on Cinema*. New York: Bordighera Press.

_____. 2002. *Italian/American Short Films & Videos: A Semiotic Reading*. West Lafayette: Purdue University Press.

_____. 1995. "What Is [Not] Italian/American about *Lena's Spaghetti*?" *Voices in Italian Americana* 6.1: 169-82.

_____. 1994. "In (Re)cognition of the Italian/American Writer: Definitions and Categories." *Differentia, review of italian thought* 6/7 (Spring/Autumn): 9-32.

Turner, Victor. 1969. *The Ritual Process. Structure and Antistructure*. Chicago: Aldine.

A Conclusion

My overall intention in assembling this modest-sized book was to guide my reader through a series of analyses of Italian/American films that have enjoyed, each in its own way, a certain aesthetic reputation for their respective uniqueness.[1] In so doing, I wanted to demonstrate how each of these films can be read on different levels in a general sense, on the one hand. With regard to the Italian/American component, in turn, I wanted to show how these films can seem to signify things that might get lost in one person's viewing, so to speak, whereas another viewer — one who is of Italian origin or has an intimate familiarity with Italian/American culture — might better be able to navigate these interpretive waters and hence arrive at a greater opportunity of interpretive choices.

We saw, for instance, how the rhetoric of each film might imply and/or suggest other modes of sign reading — i.e., interpretation of imagery — that may not be readily visible to the general spectator. I have in mind the opening of *Nuovomondo*, which I discussed in chapter one. A rock initially perceived as part of mountain for the first few seconds it appears soon turns out to be what it is, a rock, when we see Salvatore's hand appear. Then, of course, there is America, which neither the immigrants or us as spectators ever see in this film. Indeed, it is perceived though fog only, similar to the fog in Calvino's *Marcovaldo*; in each case it figures as a blank space on which to project — pun intended — a concept. Namely, the windows at Ellis Island are also foggy, but even before, as the boat arrived in New York bay, as we noted above, there was too much fog to decipher the shoreline.[2]

---

[1] While each of these films has enjoyed a positive critical reception, none was a box-office hit. They each grossed, at best, modest figures which did not even meet the basic requirements of the costs of making the films. *Nuovomondo* grossed $7,228,273; *Big Night* grossed $12,008,376; *Dinner Rush* grossed under $1,000,000; and *Mean Streets* grossed $3,000,000.

[2] The only exception is Salvatore and two other immigrants who succeed in momentarily seeing New York City when they climb to the top of the large window. Otherwise, America exists beyond the fog and, in similar fashion, on the other side of the opaque windows in Ellis Island.

And so, as we accompany Salvatore and his group on their journey, we also come to understand that, more than place, it is the concept "America" and all that it pertains that they are seeking and that they come to find/perceive and hence appropriate. Such conceptualization is ultimately signaled by the fog, which began with such a specific semiotic function, I would underscore, on the ship midway across the ocean. At a certain point, the flirtation and gradual relationship that grows between Lucy and Salvatore congeals at one of the foggiest moments on board, when they discuss marriage.

Up to this juncture in the film, it was Lucy who seemed to guide the Mancusos. Now, instead, it is Salvatore who literally lives up to his name, as he will *save*, so to speak, Lucy, as well as those who travelled with him. He has at this point conceived, perceived, and ultimately comprehended what it means to go to America—namely, to arrive at an understanding of a way of life different and more fruitful than what he had before. Yes, *Nuovomondo* is about the trials and tribulations of emigration and all that it pertains, undoubtedly. But the film is also about the perceptual aspect of emigration, one recognizing the practicalities of it while at the same time coming to the realization that there are conceptual aspects that are equally if not more significant than the physical.

In both *Big Night* and *Dinner Rush* we saw how food is a clear marker, especially, for the notion of old world vs. new world and, as well, for identity, both personal and societal. In the first instance of old world versus new world, notions of what it means to be American as opposed to what if means to be Italian are, banally speaking, up front and in our face. We see this in the film-long discussion between Primo and Secondo, for example, and the former's stridency not to compromise his cuisine. As we saw, this obstinance on Primo's part also goes against the conceptual grain of thought that Italian immigrants were more the docile and conciliatory types of individuals, especially in their interactions with the American society at large. Primo refuses to compromise; Secondo is all about compromise; and, last but not least, Pascal manifests the immigrant's total desire to become part and parcel of the American way. In teasing out these differences of Italian identity, the sign /food/

and all of its conceptual components constitute the requisite platform for such a discussion.

Dinner Rush, on the other hand, brings us into a notably different semiosphere for these two over-riding themes. Old world vs. new world is more generally articulated by the very fact of the film's thematics of being Italian in the United States. More significant here, instead, is the dialectics of identity *within* an Italian milieu — a specifically ethnic semiosphere, that is. This is the major difference between these two films on food. While *Big Night* is externally focused vis-à-vis Italian identity, *Dinner Rush* deals with the notion of Italian identity from an internal dialectic. The distinction is, in turn, both generational and somatic. The generational is manifested by the many discussions between Louis the father and Udo the son that we witness throughout the film. Food and small-town organized crime are the foundation upon which the film articulates such differences. The opening lunch scene does both: the appearance of the type of food, and the discussion between Louis and Enrico, set the stage. In turn, the subsequent murder of Enrico then sets into motion the rest of the film, as we saw. References such as "the Godfather's table" and Black and Blue dining at Gigino's continually remind us of this aspect of generational difference. Udo simply wants no part of it. He says to Louis early on, "Why don't you stick with the bookmaking and let me run this business?"

The somatic aspect of Italian identity is problematized through the character of Duncan. As we saw what Rebecca West had articulated back in 1991, Duncan's presence within this Italian semiosphere reminds us of the importance of socio-cultural context and its impact on an individual's identity. The long-term conditions of a person's life, the daily microenvironment in which one lives and carries out her/his consequential activities, can readily define one's identity: in this case, it becomes a sense of identity that is internally generated by the individual him/herself, not by some external demographic. This became clear as we teased out this notion through the lens of Peirce's tripartite notion of the sign through its firstness, secondness, and thirdness. That said, from a methodological perspective, we now see how the elasticity of relevance of the significance of Peirce's notions of firstness, secondness, and thirdness proved effi-cacious both with regard to the three "Italians" and their phases of identity in *Big Night* as it subsequently did with regard to *Dinner Rush*, this time with regard to identity and a person's daily microen-vironment and not her/his natal heritage.

My insistence on differential analytical methodologies and the possibility of added interpretations to seemingly fixed signs comes to pass, for the moment, in the final chapter dedicated to *Mean Streets*. Among the four films examined herein, Scorsese's film is, in my opinion, the most semiotically productive. Whatever any direc-tor's intentions might have been in making a film, here Scorsese has assembled a film whose significatory potentiality is greater, I would submit, than most Italian/American films. It is thus through the lens of unlimited semiosis that we can generate a plethora of meanings ("interpretants," Peirce would tell us) from such a rich inventory of signs. For this very reason, it is no coincidence that this film comes last in the sequence of chapters. My point here, as I have done in similar situations in the past with regard to the literary text (1990, 1994), is that a sign may surely generate more meaning than we initially realize once it comes into contact with a reader/viewer. This is surely the case with *Mean Streets*, as I have rehearsed in the fourth chapter of this volume. For instance, while numerous critics have spoken of Scorsese's use of music in this film, I am unaware of anyone speaking to the specifics of *Jumpin' Jack Flash* and Johnny Boy's sociopathic personality. In that Pericean act of unlimited semiosis (Eco) and its requisite reconciliation with the text, we saw how one can arrive at such a significatory end and to what degree.

Another issue that arose out of my analysis of *Mean Streets* is one of those seemingly ever-present issues that no one seems to address in any profound manner. I am speaking to the notion of the "in-formed Italian/American spectator" (reader if in terms of the written text). There are various semiotic circumstances in which one's know-ledge or lack thereof of Italian and/or Italian/American culture will determine either the fullness or the sketchiness of a spectator's com-prehension of a film or any part of it. In *Mean Streets*, we saw how, through the practice of code-switching, a character can be at a loss for a greater understanding of the specific circumstance. More relevant to the issue at hand, we also understood how the viewer — indeed, the professional critic as well — may not arrive at that deeper level of conceptual adequacy if s/he does not understand Italian, or some pidgin form of it, to a certain degree.

My point here was not to create any form of hierarchy with regard to interpretation theory. Nor did I want to engage in any form of ethnic-intellectual exclusion by implying that one need be of Italian ancestry to understand an Italian/American film. Instead, my fundamental point was, and remains, that one's semiotic cultural reservoir is elemental in how we interpret any form of textual communication; cinematic, written, bi- and/or tridimensional.[3] Ultimately, as we approach a text, all those elements that reside within our semiotic cultural reservoir, what we know at the moment of consumption of said text, allows us the privilege to engage, to a greater degree, in that Peircean notion of unlimited semiosis and, hopefully, arrive at an even greater interpretive comprehension of the text at hand.

WORKS CITED

Calvino, Italo. 1963. *Marcovaldo, ovvero le stagioni in città*, with illustrations by Sergio Tofano (Turin: Einaudi. In English, *Marcovaldo: Or the Seasons in the City*. Tr. William Weaver. New York: Harcourt Brace Jovanovich, 1983.

Eco, Umberto. 1976. *A Theory of Semiotics.* Bloomington: Indiana University Press.

Peirce, Charles Sanders. 1931-1935. *The Collected Papers of Charles Sanders Peirce*. Vols. I-VI Charles Hartshorne and Paul Weiss, eds. Cambridge, MA: Harvard University Press.

Tamburri, Anthony Julian. 2021. "Italian Diaspora Studies and the University: Professional Development and Curricular Matters" in *"This*

---

[3] In a different venue this might lead us to the more overriding and decades-long issue of how non-Italian Americans continue to perceive Italian Americans. From the early imagery at the turn of the twentieth century to some of the latest depictions of late, stereotypes continue to abound. At this juncture, a collateral conversation would, indeed should, be dedicated to what Italian Americans themselves might do about such depictions beyond the proverbial letter of protest. I have dealt with this issue in two current essays (2020, 2021).

Hope Sustains the Scholar": Essays in Tribute to the Work of Robert Viscusi. Siân Gibby, Joseph U. Sciorra, Anthony Julian Tamburri, eds. New York: Boridghera Press.

_____. 2020. The Semiotics of Labeling: 'Italian' to 'American,' 'Non-white' to 'White,' and Other Privileges of Choosing" in Susanna Nanni and Sabrina Vellucci, eds. *Circolazione di persone e di idee.* New York: Bordighera Press. 1-18.

_____. 1994. "In (Re)cognition of the Italian/American Writer: Definitions and Categories." *Differentia, review of italian thought* 6/7 (Spring/Autumn): 9-32.

_____. 1990. "Aldo Palazzeschi's :*riflessi.* Toward a Notion of a 'Retro-Lector'." *The American Journal of Semiotics.* 7.1/2: 105-24.

West, Rebecca. 1991. "Scorsese's *Who's That Knocking At My Door?* Night Thoughts on Italian Studies in the United States." *Romance Languages Annual.* Ben Lawton and Anthony Julian Tamburri, eds. 331-338.

Aaron, Daniel, 52, 52–53n6
all and nothing signification, 30, 30nn14–15
ambiguity. *See* liminality / ambiguity
Americanization, 54, 56, 64–65, 68–70. *See also* "the apathetic reaction"; "the rebel reaction"
androgyne metaphor, 84–85
Angelo Mancuso (*Nuovomondo*), 15–17
Anne (*Big Night*), 59
anthropological method (Feyerbrand), 9n10
    "the apathetic reaction" (Child)
    in *Big Night*, 53, 60
    characteristics, 52–53, 55–56
    in *Dinner Rush*, 88, 91
Arnheim, Rudolf, 1
assassination scene (*Dinner Rush*), 85–86

Barolini, Helen, 32n18
basement, as sign, 85, 85–86n9
Bassetti, Piero, 90n12, 91, 98n5
Bazan, Andre, 3
Being and Nothingness (Sartre), 6
Benamou, Michel, 3
Berstein, Richard, 9n10
Big Night (Scott and Tucci)
    dichotomies in, 52, 70
    and the Louis Prima character, 70–71
    main characters, 51
    old world/new world perceptual differences, 52, 57–58, 60–62

rebirth in, 69–70
    See also food, Italian
biological determinism, 38
blank space, 8–10, 113
Bondanella, Peter, 3–4
Bordighera Press, 95
Borzello, Frances, 2

Cadillac, as sign, 63–64
Calabretta Sajder, Ryan, 75
Calvino, Italo, 7–9, 113
Camaiti Hostert, Anna, 59, 62, 62–63n17, 68n20
Campisi, Paul, 52–53n6
Catholicism, 31n6, 62–63n17, 63, 99n7
Cavallero, Jonathan, 100n8, 102
celebrity
    in *Big Night*, 67, 70–71
    in *Dinner Rush*, 76, 78, 84n8
cervello (brains), 103–4
Charlie (*Mean Streets*)
    code-switching by, 105–7
    devotion to St. Francis of Assisi, 107
    during Johnny Boy's entry, 97, 99–103
    greeting of Johnny Boy, 103–4
    inability to save Johnny Boy, 108
    racism, 104–5, 107
    See also Mean Streets
Child, Irvin L., 52, 60, 64, 69, 88–89
class signs
    in *Big Night*, 63–64
    in *Mean Streets*, 102, 108
    in *Nuovomundo*, 21–25, 29–33, 37

cognition, 2, 52–56, 54n10,
56n11. *See also* Italian/
American identity
color and light signs
in *Big Night*, 66–67
in *Dinner Rush*, 77–78
in *Mean Streets*, 66n19, 107
in *Nuovomundo*, 16–17, 21,
25, 35
Western vs. Eastern symbolism, 21n6
in "The Wrong Stop," 7–9
Cometa, Michele, 90–91
Crialese, Emanuele, 15–17, 19.
See also Nuovomundo (Crialese)

de Saussure, Ferdinand, 2
Diane (*Mean Streets*), 104–5
Dinner Rush (Giraldi)
assassination scene, 85–96
food as performance, 76
and the linking of food and
organized crime, 79, 86
juxtaposition of contemporary and traditional
food, 77
old world/new world dichotomy, 73, 75–79, 87–88
plot, 75
semiotics of final scene, 88
three types of Italians, 88
Dolores Torres (*Nuovomundo*),
39–40, 39–40n23
Dondis, Donis A., 2, 4, 6–7
Duncan (*Dinner Rush*)
as an "apathetic" Italian,
88–89, 91
food produced by, 77
relationship with Nicole,
83–84

relationship with Udo, 80–
82
role in the performance, 80
semiotic function, 78–80

Eco, Umberto, 40n25, 116
education, and status, 54, 61, 65
effective identity, 98, 98n5
emigration
conceptual aspects, 30–31,
32n17, 114
immigration vs., 22
and in-between-ness, 29
and "the journey," 29–30,
45–47
and transnationalism, 22–
23n7
See also liminali-
ty/ambiguity; old
world/ new world di-
chotomy
Enrico (*Dinner Rush*), 78, 115

feeble-mindedness, 41, 41n26
Fellini, Federico, 99n7
Feyerabend, Paul, 9n10
film/movies
academic approaches, 3
and filling in blanks, voids,
blocks, 8–10
influence on social mores,
10
informed vs. specialized
viewer, 10
meaning of, role of spectator and filmmaker, 6
movement as dominant
visual element, 4–5
and the movie-going expe-
rience, 7
Film Theory and Criticism, 3

Fiore, Teresa, 23n7
"firstness" (Peirce), 53–55, 54n7.
    See also "the in-group reaction
fog, semiotic function, 8–9, 16,
    40n24, 113–14
food, Italian
    as identity, 73
    meals, traditional, 51n2
    old world/ new world per-
        ceptual differences, 77,
        79–80, 87–88
    preparing, 57 –58, 76–77, 79
    "sausage and peppers," 75–
        76, 80, 91
    and sexuality, 82
    sign functions, 75
    "spaghetti and meatballs,"
        56–58, 60, 66–67, 76
    See also Americanization;
        Italian/ American iden-
        tity; old world new
        world dichotomy
food nymph (*Dinner Rush*), 82–
    83
Fortunata Mancuso (*Nuovomon-
    do*), 17–19, 18n2, 28–29,
    34n19, 36–38, 41–45
Foucault, Michael, 6
Francis of Assisi, Saint, 107

Gabriella (*Big Night*), 62–63,
    63n18, 65, 68
Gadamer, Hans-Georg, 9n10
"the gaze" (Sartre), 6
Geertz, Clifford, 9n10
gender. *See* women/ gender re-
    lationships
Giraldi, Bob. *See Dinner Rush*
    (Giraldi)
The Godfather (Coppola), 73, 86

Goodfellas (Scorsese), 73
Greco, Joseph, 95, 95n2
Green, Rose Basile, 52n5

Herbie (*Lena's Spaghetti*), 97n4
hermeneutic circle, 9n10
Heyer-Caput, Margherita, 22n7
A History of Italian Cinema (Bon-
    danella), 4
*Hollywood's Italian American
    Filmmakers: Capra, Scorsese,
    Savoca, Coppola, and Taranti-
    no* (Cavallero), 102
homoerotic signs, 85
hyphenated nomenclature, 52,
    52–53nn5–6

"the in-group reaction" (Child),
    52–55, 88. *See also* "firstness"
    (Peirce)
"intentio lectoris" (Eco), 25
Iser, Wolfgang, 8–9, 96n3
ISSNAF (Italian Scientists and
    Scholars in North America
    Foundation), 74
Italian/ American identity
    confusion about, 25–26
    definitions, 88–90
    effective identity, 98–99,
        98n5
    exclusionary impulses, 74
    generational differences,
        52–53nn5–6, 91–92, 95
    and hyphenated nomencla-
        ture, 52, 52–53nn5–6
    and immigrant narratives,
        24
    and *italianità* concept, 89–90,
        90n12, 98–99
    as a mosaic/ progression of
        identities, 68n20, 52–56,

56n11, , 68n20, 73–75, 90–92
See also food, Italian; organized crime *and specific films*
Italian/American spectators, as informed viewers, 12, 57, 98–99, 102–8,
italianità concept, 89–90, 90n12, 98–99
I vitelloni (Fellini), 99n7

Jennifer Freely (*Dinner Rush*), 80–82
Johnny Boy Civello (*Mean Streets*)
    bar scene with "girlfriends," 99–101
    Charlie's greeting of, 103–4
    inherent violence/chaos of, 101–2, 104n10
    See also Mean Streets
Ken Roloff (*Dinner Rush*), 76–77, 86–87
Keyser, Les, 97–98, 103n9
kitchen, as sign, 68, 76–78, 82–83, 85–86n9, 87, 89
Kolker, Philip, 97–98, 99n6, 101

language, spoken
    in *Dinner Rush*, 86
    and extra-textual meaning, 18–19, 18–19n4
    in *Mean Streets*, 103–4, 106–8, 106n11
    in *Nuovomondo*, 26–28, 28n12, 32, 35, 43–44
Lena's Spaghetti (Greco), 95–96, 97n4
liminality/ambiguity, 24, 30, 36, 40, 81, 96–97

literacy, 17–18, 18n4, 28–29
Lombroso, Cesare, 38
Lopreato, Joseph, 52–53n6, 53–56
Louis (*Dinner Rush*), 77–78, 88–89
Lucy (*Nuovomondo*)
    contrast with the Mancuso family, 22
    liminality, in-betweenness, 29, 35–36
    as a Peircian sign, 30, 45
    relationship with Fortunata, 36
    relationship with Salvatore, 32–35
    See also Nuovomundo
Lyotard, Jean-François, 75, 109

Marcovaldo ("The Wrong Stop")
    movie-going experience, 7–9
    and the function of fog, 40n24
    meals. *See* food, Italian
Mean Streets (Scorsese)
    ambiguity of opening sequences, 97
    code-switching in, 103–8, 106n11
    color symbolism, 66n19, 107
    emotional deprivation theme, 100
    ethnic degradation/racism in, 103–6, 103n9
    Franciscan paradox, 107–8
    issues of randomness/disconnectedness, 99–100
    Johnny Boy's entry scene, 99–102

name of the bar, 107–8
revisiting signification of, 97
slow motion effects, 101
Merrell, Floyd, 30n15, 69n22
Milli Konewko, Simone, 22–23n7
Mimì metallurgico ferito nell'onore, 34
movement, film as, 4–6
Mulvey, Laura, 6
mutism, selective, 43
Myers-Scotton, Carol, 106n11

names, as signs, 51, 64, 67, 77, 103
The New Art History (ed. Rees and Borzello), 2
nicknames, 77
Nicola Esposito (*Nuovomondo*), 26
Nicole (*Dinner Rush*), 76, 81–84
"nothing," Peirce's concept, 68–69, 68n21
Nuovomondo (Crialese)
    arrival and examination scenes, 37–38
    birds-eye views in, 46
    class contrasts, 22
    color symbolism, 35
    dead infant scene, 31–32
    departure scene, 20–23, 25
    final scene, 42
    focus on the journey, 22, 29
    hair-combing scene, 32
    images conveying skepticism, 19
    old world/ new world dichotomies, 17, 38–42
    opening scene, 16
    river of milk images, 33–34, 34n19, 42, 45–47

Simone's "Sinnerman" in, 47
    and skepticism about language, 17–18, 17–18n4, 26–29
    stone imagery, 20–21
    storm scene, 31
    sur-reality of, 22
    use of contrast, 15

old world/new world dichotomy
    in *Big Night*, 52, 57–58, 60–62
    in *Dinner Rush*, 77, 87–88
    in *Mean Streets*, 105
    in *Nuovomundo*, 15, 17, 38–42
organized crime, semiotic role, 73, 79, 86–87, 95, 108, 115

Panofsky, Erwin, 1–2, 4–6, 10
Paolo (*Dinner Rush*), 78, 82, 86
"Paradiso," as sign, 62
Pascal (*Big Night*)
    Americanization, 64–67, 69–70
    manifestation of "the rebel" reaction, 64
    naming of self and restaurant, 64
    as representative of "the rebel reaction," 53–54, 62
    triangle with Primo and Secondo, 51, 67
    See also Big Night
Pascali, Lara, 85–86n9
Peirce, Charles Sanders
    concept of "nothing," 68–69, 68n21
    concept of "the real," 54n10
    firstness, secondness, and thirdness, 54
    focus on logic and cognition, 2

ideas, among the universes of experience, 69n23
and the process of developing cognition, 56
sign representamen, 5–6, 6n5
and sign representamen, 30
three cognitive categories, 52–53, 54
perceptual psychology, 1–2
performance
and relationship of performer and audience, 80–82
as theme in *Dinner Rush*, 76–79
Phyliis (*Big Night*), 62–63, 62–63n17
Pietro Mancuso (*Nuovomondo*)
fears and loss of immigrant identity, 24
interrelationship with Pietro and speech, 40–44
"*pisciare*," multiple meanings for, in *Dinner Rush*, 86–87
pre-filmic phenomena, 7
Prima, Louis, absence of, in *Big Night*, 70–71
A Primer of Visual Literary (Dondis), 2
Primo (*Big Night*)
name, 51
refusal to compromise, 65, 68
ties to Italian identity, 53, 56–60
See also Big Night
Principles of Philosophy (Peirce), 54
Purdue University Annual Conference on Film, 3–4

racism, in *Mean Streets*, 105–7
reality
"actual" vs. semiotic, 69n22
of ideas, 69n23
Peirce's definition, 54n10
and spectator expectations, 7
"the rebel reaction" (Child), 52–56, 64, 88, 91
Rees, A. L., 2
re-reading, 96n3
"risotto," 60–62. *See also* food, Italian
Rita and Rosa (*Nuovomundo*), 17–18, 32, 32n17, 36–37, 39
river of milk image (*Nuovomundo*), 33–34, 34n19, 42, 45–47

Sajder, Calabretta, 82
Salvatore Mancuso (*Nuovomondo*)
departure scene imagery, 20–21
innocence, provincialism, and confusion about Italian identity and, 25–27
opening scene of struggle and sacrifice, 15–17
postcards inviting emigration, 17
relationship with Lucy, 32–35
"rising to the top" imagery, 23, 24n8
See also Nuovomundo
Sartre, Jean Paul, 6
sausage and peppers. *See* food, Italian
Scorsese, Martin, 66n19, 97,

99n7. *See also Mean Streets*
secondness (practicality, "experience"), 54–55, 54n8, 60. *See also* "the apathetic reaction" (Child)
Secondo (*Big Night*)
  focus on survival, 60, 61
  naming of, 51
  need to compromise, 68
  new-world adventurism, 53, 57–58, 60
  relationships with Phyllis and Gabriella, 62
  relationships with women, 62–64
  See also Big Night
semiotics
  as interpretive approach, 1
  names, nomenclature, 51
  and retrospective reading, 86n10
  semiotic knots, 30, 36
  and signs, signifiers, 11, 30, 30nn14–15
  underlying concepts, 2
  on "unlimited semiosis," 40n25
Sicily, as the old world, 15, 21n6
  signs, signification
  all and nothing, 30, 30nn14–15
  and the androgyne metaphor, 84–85
  and filling in blanks, voids, blocks, 8–10
  and the importance of the visual, 16–18
  and individualized interpretation, 5–6, 6n5
  for informed/casual viewers, 10–12

of "Italian American" and "Italian," 73–75, 77
  of old and new worlds, 36, 45–46
  pre-filmic phenomena, 7
  relationship to the object, 5–6
  re-reading in *Mean Streets*, 97
  role of sign functions, 1
  and the symbiotic relationships, 80–82
  and taking one sign for another, 27–28
  See also spectatorship *and specific films*
Simone, Nina, 47
spaghetti and meatballs. *See* food, Italian
spectatorship
  film vs. theater, 4–5
  informed vs. specialized viewer, 8–12, 96–97, 96n3, 98–99, 103–7
  and the interplay between the local and the global, 8–10, 9n10
  and interpretation, 98, 109
  the "moviegoer," 10n11
  and pre-filmic phenomena, 7
  and role of filmmakers, 6
  and signification, 5–7, 12
  and subliminal references, 96
  as theme in *Dinner Rush*, 77, 77n6
  See also Italian/American spectators; signification *and specific films*
"Subliminal Ethnicity: What is

[not] Italian/ American about *Lena's Spaghetti?"* (Tamburri), 96
Symposium (Plato), 84–85

thirdness (rationality, thought), 53, 54n9, 55–56
Tony (*Mean Streets*), 99n6, 101
Turner, Victor, 96

Udo (*Dinner Rush*)
    choice of celebrity, 84n8
    conflicting identities, 76
    and the importance of food preparation, 77
    as "the rebel," 77, 88–89
    relationship with Nicole, 83–84
    relationship with Duncan, 80–82
    See also Dinner Rush
Umbertina (Baroloni), 32n18
Ury, William, 106n11

Virga, Anita, 23n7
visual communication

as field of study, 1
and film as art form, 4
relationship with language/ speech, 18–19, 18–19n4, 27–28
See also signification

West, Rebecca, 89–91
Who's That Knocking at My Door? (Scorsese), 62–63
women/ gender relationships
    in *Big Night*, 62
    in *Dinner Rush*, 84n8, 85n9
    Lucy as representative of in *Nuovomundo*, 30, 32–35
    in *Mean Streets*, 100–101, 103–6
    in *Nuovomondo*, 25, 28, 36–39, 39–40n23
    and objectification, 6
    and the treatment at Ellis Island, 37
    and virginity in wives to be, 62–63
"The Wrong Stop" (Calvino), 7–9

Zavala, Lauro, 7n7, 10, 10n11

ABOUT THE AUTHOR

ANTHONY JULIAN TAMBURRI is Dean of the John D. Calandra Italian American Institute, a university-wide research institute under the aegis of Queens College of The City University of New York, and Distinguished Professor of European Languages and Literatures.

In addition to his fourteen authored books and more than 120 peer-reviewed essays, he has edited more than forty volumes. With Paolo A. Giordano and Fred L. Gardaphé, he is contributing co-editor of the volume *From The Margin: Writings in Italian Americana* (1991; 2nd edition, 2000), and co-founder of Bordighera Press, the publisher of *Voices in Italian Americana, Italiana,* and four book series, as well as the LAURIA/FRASCA POETRY PRIZE. Other co-edited volumes include, *Beyond the Margin: Readings in Italian Americana* (1998), *Screening Ethnicity: Cinematographic Representations of Italian Americans in the United States* (2002), *The Representation of the Mediterranean World by Insiders and Outsiders* (2018), *Mediterranean Encounters and Clashes: Incontri e scontri mediterranei* (2020), *This Hope Sustains the Scholar: Essays in Tribute to the Work of Robert Viscusi* (2021), *Il miglior fabbro: Essays in Honor of Joseph Tusiani* (2021), and *Diversity in Italian Studies* (2021).

Tamburri's degrees are from Southern Connecticut State University (BS, Italian), Middlebury College (MA, Italian), U.C. Berkeley (PhD, Italian). He first taught in high-school, and subsequently went to Smith College, Middlebury College, Auburn University, and Purdue University, before moving to Florida Atlantic University where he served as Chair of Languages and Linguistics, then Associate Dean for Research, Graduate, and Interdisciplinary Studies, as well as the director of the PhD Program in Comparative Studies. He is past president of the American Italian Historical Association (now Italian American Studies Association) and the American Association of Teachers of Italian. He is also executive producer of the TV program *Italics*.

Among his honors, he was named Distinguished Alumnus in 2000 by Southern Connecticut State University; in 2008, then Bronx President Adolfo Carrion awarded him the Certificate of Appreciation for work as educator and community leader for Italian Americans; and, in 2010 he was conferred the honor of *Cavaliere dell'Ordine al Merito della Repubblica Italiana*; and the "Frank Stella Person of the Year Award," ILICA. Other awards include: "The Lehman-LaGuardia Award for

Civic Achievement." Commission for Social Justice Order Sons of Italy (New York State) in America and B'nai B'rith International (Metro-North Region) (2011); the AATI Award for Distinguished Service for Colleges and Universities (2013); the "Leonard Covello Award for Distinguished Service" of the Italian Teachers Association of New York (2013); The Joseph Coccia Jr. Heritage, Language and Culture Award for exceptional efforts by word and deed in promoting and preserving our Italian Heritage, Language or Culture. UNICO National (2016); National Council of Columbia Associations, "Man of The Year" Award (2017).

Made in the USA
Middletown, DE
06 September 2021